Cupid's Arrow

The Course of Love through Time

Cupid's Arrow

The Course of Love through Time

Robert J. Sternberg
Yale University

CAMBRIDGE
UNIVERSITY PRESS

PUBLISHED BY THE PRESS SYNDICATE OF THE UNIVERSITY OF CAMBRIDGE
The Pitt Building, Trumpington Street, Cambridge CB2 1RP, United Kingdom

CAMBRIDGE UNIVERSITY PRESS
The Edinburgh Building, Cambridge CB2 2RU, UK   htttp://www.cup.cam.ac.uk
40 West 20th Street, New York, NY 10011-4211, USA   http://www.cup.org
10 Stamford Road, Oakleigh, Melbourne 3166, Australia

© Cambridge University Press 1998

First published 1998

Printed in the United States of America

Typeset in Sabon 10/13 pt, in Quark XPress™ [AG]

*The catalog record for this book is available from
the British Library.*

Library of Congress Cataloging-in-Publication Data
Sternberg, Robert J.
Cupid's arrow : the course of love through time / Robert J. Sternberg.
p.   cm.
Includes indexes.
ISBN 0-521-47320-9 (hardcover).
1. Love.   I. Title.
BL575.L8S7754   1998
152.4'1—dc21   97-52933
                                                                                    CIP

ISBN 0-521-47320-9 hardback

Contents

v

Part V.   When Cupid's Arrow Falls:
Love in Our Lifetime: Endings

Preface

Psyche was the youngest daughter of three daughters of a great king. So beautiful was she in both countenance and spirit that people traveled from all over the world to admire her. Venus, goddess of beauty, became jealous of Psyche because their admiration of Psyche led people to neglect and even forget about Venus. So Venus devised a plot: She asked her son, Cupid, the god of love, to make Psyche fall in love with the most detestable creature in the whole world. This should have been an easy task for Cupid, whose arrows of love could make people fall in love with anyone Cupid chose for them.

Cupid arranged for Psyche to be abandoned by her parents on a hilltop, where she would be betrothed to an ugly and vile winged serpent. Psyche wept at her fate but was resigned to her doom because, although she was beautiful, no one had in fact fallen in love with her, and so it seemed that only the winged serpent would have her.

Venus had not counted on one detail, though, a crucial detail when it comes to love. Cupid, upon seeing Psyche, himself fell in love with her. Instead of bringing her a monster, he spirited her to his magnificent palace and made her his wife. However, because Psyche was a mortal, Cupid could not allow her to know either who he was or what he looked like. He visited her only at night and made her agree never to look upon him. Psyche lived a happy life with Cupid, although one of mystery.

Eventually, Psyche's sisters, upon seeing the splendid palace where Psyche lived, became envious and devised a plot to ruin her. They poisoned her mind, assuring Psyche that if her husband was so secretive about his identity and appearance, there must be something wrong with him. Clearly, they said, Psyche had ended up with the dreadful winged serpent after all.

Psyche finally could no longer bear the uncertainty of not knowing who her husband was or what he looked like. One night, while Cupid slept, Psyche cautiously carried a lamp to his bed to gaze upon his face. Instead of seeing a monster, however, she saw as handsome a face as one could possibly imagine, and her hands started to tremble at the sight of her beloved husband. As she trembled, though, oil fell from her lamp and severely burned Cupid's shoulder. He awoke and, finding that his wife had betrayed him, he fled.

In anguish at her faithlessness and at having hurt him and then lost him, Psyche vowed to show Cupid how much she loved him by spending the rest of her life searching for him. She prayed to all the gods for help, but none of them wanted to risk the wrath of Venus. Finally, in desperation, Psyche prayed to Venus herself.

Cupid had flown to his mother and asked her to treat his wound. When Venus heard that Cupid had married Psyche and that Psyche had betrayed her pledge to Cupid, Venus decided to punish Psyche severely. When Psyche begged for forgiveness from Venus, Venus belittled Psyche as faithless and plain and told her that her only hope of forgiveness was to perform certain tasks. The tasks were clearly impossible, but Psyche hoped that in her travels to complete the tasks she might find her lost love. First, Venus took some tiny seeds of wheat, poppy, and millet, mixed them, and dropped them in a single pile. She gave Psyche until nightfall to separate the seeds. Psyche despaired, but a colony of ants, showing compassion, sorted them for her. Venus returned and, seeing what had happened, became even angrier.

So Venus gave Psyche more impossible tasks, such as to fetch the golden wool of some fierce sheep and to obtain black water from the river of the dead, the Styx. Each time, Venus was certain that Psyche would not be able to fulfill the task set out for her. But each time, through the help of others, Psyche fulfilled her tasks. Finally Cupid, who was now healed, longed for her once again. He went to her, scolded her gently for her earlier faithlessness, and assured her that her search was over. He longed to reunite with her, so he approached Jupiter, the king of the gods, and beseeched him to grant Psyche immortality. Jupiter consented and, before an assembly of gods, made Psyche a goddess and announced that Cupid and Psyche were formerly married. Even Venus was joyous. Her son now had a suitable match. Moreover, with Psyche in the heavens rather than on Earth, people would no longer be distracted by Psyche's beauty and would worship Venus again.

It is fitting to name a book on love in honor of Cupid, because the story of Cupid and Psyche has so many of the elements of love stories past and present: desire, mystery, beauty, confusion, search, jealousy, faith, faithlessness, forgiveness, assistance from others, resistance from others, angry parents, and repentance, among others. Most of all, it is fitting that Cupid – he who shot the arrows of love – should himself have fallen in love unexpectedly. *The goal of this book is to follow the course of Cupid's arrow. The book is about love over time: over historical time, over life's time, over love's time.*

This book is written for anyone who wants to learn about and understand love. The book is grounded in my own "triangular theory" of love, which, in Part I, sets the basis for the rest of the book. In this part, I discuss the composition of Cupid's arrow, describe the three components of the triangular theory (Chapter 1), the seven kinds of love generated by the three components (Chapter 2), how the three components form into different triangles of love and how these triangles of love develop over time (Chapter 3), and how love as characterized by the triangular theory can be measured (Chapter 4). These concepts, introduced in my earlier book, *The Triangle of Love,* are used throughout the present book. This book draws and builds on the earlier one, but it is not limited to an exposition of just the one theory. The theory in this book is distinguished from the theory in my book, *Love Is a Story,* which deals with how people come to form the triangles they have through stories about what love should be.

In Part II, I consider the aiming of Cupid's arrow: the conceptions people have had of love throughout the ages, as it has been revealed in many lifetimes. Part II starts with the prehistory of love (Chapter 5), and continues with the history of love as revealed both by culture (Chapter 6) and by literature (Chapter 7).

In Part III, I discuss the firing of Cupid's arrow – how love begins in our own lifetime. I discuss the role of childhood and adolescence (Chapter 8) and of adulthood (Chapter 9) in the formation of our preferences for the kind of person to whom we will be attracted.

In Part IV, I discuss Cupid's arrow in flight as well as when it strikes – how we find love in our lifetimes and how it continues through our lifetimes, its middles. This part of the book deals with both a key mechanism for ensuring the durability of relationships, reward (Chapter 10), and the course of relationships (Chapter 11).

Finally, in Part V, I consider what happens when Cupid's arrow falls to the ground and relationships end. In this part, I deal with both decay (Chapter 12) and dissolution of relationships, as well as with their rebirth (Chapter 13).

I am grateful to Julia Hough for contracting the book for Cambridge and for her careful editing of the book. I also thank Anne E. Beall, who coauthored the material in Chapter 6, and Susan Hayden, who coauthored the material in Chapter 7. My other collaborators in my love research, Susan Grajek, Michael Barnes, Sandra Wright, and Mahzad Hojjat, have also been invaluable in the development of my thinking about love. Finally, I thank all those in my life who have contributed to my understanding of love.

Names and identifying information in all vignettes told in this book have been changed.

PART I

The Composition of Cupid's Arrow: What Is Love?

1

A Three-Component View of Love

Jason first fell in love in the first grade. The girl, whom I will call Irene, was a classmate of his and lived right up the block. She and Jason spent a lot of time together, playing the usual childhood games, like hide and seek, tag, and house, walking to school, and helping each other out in any way they could. Irene and Jason had a modest plan: to become king and queen of the world, and to have everyone else in the world as their subjects. There was also one other detail in their plan: They would wear clothes, but no one else would be allowed to wear them. No doubt, Freud would have had a field day with them.

Irene eventually moved away, and that was the end of both the friendship and the kingdom: Jason never saw her again. The love affair was neither passionate nor, it turned out, long-lasting. But Irene and Jason had at least one critical element of love: They were close friends and shared with each other intimacies they shared with no one else. They communicated well with each other and always felt comforted in each other's presence. Although they may not have had all the components of love, they certainly had one of the most important: They cared about each other and supported each other. In short, they had an emotionally intimate relationship.

Jason next fell in love with Patti, who sat in front of him in a high school class. The very first day Jason laid eyes on her, he fell madly in love. He spent whole class periods just staring at her. He never screwed up the courage to tell her how he felt about her, however. His lack of communication was not for lack of feelings. He thought about Patti

3

almost constantly and, for a year of his life, about little else. He did his schoolwork on automatic pilot. When he would talk to other people, he would be, at most, half there, because he was secretly thinking about Patti. He would go home at the end of the day and pine away thinking about her.

The months went by, but Jason couldn't move himself to express his feelings toward her; instead, he acted coldly toward her, because he was afraid of giving himself away (which he probably did anyway). He was crushed when he discovered that Patti had fallen in love with someone else. To make matters worse, the boy was a star athlete, and Jason wasn't even on a team. It all looked so bleak.

Eventually, Jason got over his obsession with Patti, and they even became somewhat friendly, although Jason discovered that he liked her less than he had loved her. Even worse, the more he got to know her, the less he felt they had in common.

The feeling Jason had for Patti was a second ingredient of love: passion. Whereas the intimacy he felt toward Irene had been mutual, as intimacy almost has to be, the passion he felt for Patti was one-sided, as passion often is. Looking back, he would call his love for Patti an infatuation: It developed without his even knowing Patti and continued in the absence of any real mutual relationship between them. Infatuation is fueled more vigorously by doubts and uncertainties than by knowledge of what a person is like. Eventually, Patti went away to college, and Jason never saw her again. Nor did he feel any great need to see her.

The third time Jason fell in love was with Cindy, whom he met relatively soon after he met Patti. His relationship with Cindy was everything his relationship with Patti was not, and vice versa. In a word, the relationship with Cindy was "sensible." They had relatively similar backgrounds and upbringings; they both did well in school and were career oriented; and, in a nutshell, they were what almost anyone would call a good match. Their relationship had neither the deep intimacy of the relationship with Irene nor the overwhelming passion of the one-sided relationship with Patti, but it did have something that the other two relationships had lacked. Cindy and Jason believed they loved each other, and so they committed themselves relatively quickly to each other.

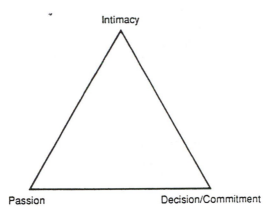

Figure 1.1. The triangle of love. The assignment of components
to vertices is one of convenience; it is arbitrary.

Paramount in each of these relationships was one of three ingredients,
or components, of love: intimacy (with Irene), passion (for Patti), and
commitment (to Cindy). Love can be understood as a triangle (which
should not be confused with a "love triangle" of three people), of which
each point is one of these three components: intimacy (the top point of
the triangle), passion (the left-hand point), and decision/commitment
(the right-hand point) (see Figure 1.1).

THE TRIANGLE OF LOVE

A substantial body of evidence suggests that the components of intimacy, passion, and commitment play a key role in love over and above
other attributes.[1] Even before I collected the first bit of data to test my
theory, I had several reasons for choosing these three components as
the building blocks for it.

First, many of the other aspects of love prove, on close examination,
to be either parts or manifestations of these three components. Communication, for example, is a building block of intimacy, as is caring or
compassion. Were one to subdivide intimacy and passion and commitment into their own subparts, the theory would eventually contain so
many elements as to become unwieldy. There is no one, solely correct

fineness of division. But a division into three components works well
in several ways, as I hope to show in this chapter and beyond.

Second, my review of the literature on couples in the United States,
as well as in other lands, suggested that, whereas some elements of love
are fairly time-bound or culture-specific, the three I propose are general across time and place. The three components are not equally
weighted in all cultures, as we will see, but each component receives
at least some weight in virtually any time or place.

Third, the three components do appear to be distinct, although, of
course, they are related. You can have any one without either or both
of the others. In contrast, other potential building blocks for a theory
of love – for example, nurturance and caring – tend to be difficult to
separate, logically as well as psychologically.

Fourth, as I will show later, many other accounts of love seem to boil
down to something similar to my own account, or a subset of it. If we
take away differences in language and tone, the spirit of many other
theories converges with mine.

Finally, and perhaps most important, the theory accounts for feelings
and behavior – as I hope to demonstrate throughout the book.

Intimacy

In the context of the triangular theory, intimacy refers to those feelings
in a relationship that promote closeness, bondedness, and connected-
ness. My research with Susan Grajek indicates that intimacy includes
at least ten elements.[2]

1. *Desiring to promote the welfare of the loved one.* The lover looks
out for the partner and seeks to promote his or her welfare. One may
promote the other's welfare at the expense of one's own – but in the
expectation that the other will reciprocate when the time comes. You
are experiencing this element when you want your partner to get the
job she wants or when you want her to get over a painful disappointment in her life.

2. *Experiencing happiness with the loved one.* The lover enjoys being with his or her partner. When they do things together, they have a
good time and build a store of memories upon which they can draw in
hard times. Furthermore, good times shared will spill over into the re-

lationship and make it better. You are experiencing this element when you are having a fantastic time with your partner on a skiing trip or at a concert.

3. *Holding the loved one in high regard.* The lover thinks highly of and respects his or her partner. Although the lover may recognize flaws in the partner, this recognition does not detract from the overall esteem in which the partner is held. You experience this element when you think your partner is the greatest, despite his failure to get a hoped-for promotion.

4. *Being able to count on the loved one in times of need.* The lover feels that the partner is there when needed. When the chips are down, the lover can call on the partner and expect that he or she will come through. You experience this feeling when the family finances are on the rocks, and your partner, who has not been working, wants to get a job immediately in order to improve them.

5. *Having mutual understanding with the loved one.* The lovers understand each other. They know each other's strengths and weaknesses and how to respond to each other in a way that shows genuine empathy for the loved one's emotional states. Each knows where the other is "coming from." You experience such understanding when you both understand, perhaps without saying a word, why the couple who has just come over to dine for the first time won't be returning – not if you can help it.

6. *Sharing oneself and one's possessions with the loved one.* One is willing to give of oneself and one's time, as well as one's things, to the loved one. Although all things need not be joint property, the lovers share their property as the need arises. And, most important, they share themselves.

7. *Receiving emotional support from the loved one.* The lover feels bolstered and even renewed by the loved one, especially in times of need. You know you have this element when you feel like nothing is going right, and you then realize that one thing is – your partner is right there with you.

8. *Giving emotional support to the loved one.* The lover supports the loved one by empathizing with, and emotionally supporting, him or her in times of need. You know you are able to give this emotional support when you feel like your partner is acting unreasonably at

work, and you still support him, whether or not you agree with his actions.

9. *Communicating intimately with the loved one.* The lover can communicate deeply and honestly with the loved one, sharing innermost feelings. This is the kind of communication that you experience when you're embarrassed by something you've done, and you still can tell your partner about it.

10. *Valuing the loved one.* The lover feels the great importance of the partner in the scheme of life. You know you have this kind of valuing when you realize that your partner is more important than the material possessions you have.

These are only some of the possible feelings one can experience through the intimacy of love; moreover, it is not necessary to experience all of these feelings in order to experience intimacy. On the contrary, our research indicates that you experience intimacy when you experience a sufficient number of these feelings, whatever the exact number may be. You do not usually experience the feelings independently, but often as one overall feeling.

What makes for intimacy? Different psychologists say similar things, albeit in different ways. Intimacy results from strong, frequent, and diverse interconnections between people.[3] The intimate couple, then, is characterized by strong ties and frequent interactions of a variety of kinds. Qualities of friendship that are keys to intimacy include trust, honesty, respect, commitment, safety, support, generosity, loyalty, mutuality, constancy, understanding, and acceptance.[4]

Intimacy probably starts in self-disclosure. To be intimate with someone, you need to break down the walls that separate one person from another. It is well known that self-disclosure begets self-disclosure: If you want to get to know what someone else is like, let him or her learn about you. But self-disclosure is often easier in same-sex friendships than in loving relationships, probably because people see themselves as having more to lose by self-disclosure in loving relationships. And odd as it may sound, spouses may be less symmetrical in self-disclosure than are strangers, again probably because the costs of self-disclosure can be so high in romantic love. Telling your lover an ugly fact about yourself may seem to you to put your relationship at risk.

One theorist has tried to put together the various findings on self-disclosure by suggesting that there is a curvilinear relationship between reciprocity and self-disclosure. The idea is that the rewards of reciprocity in self-disclosure increase up to a certain point; but when a couple becomes very intimate, the costs of self-disclosure become so great that it often will decrease, at least for one, if not both, partners.[5]

Many of us have had the experience of confiding a deep, dark secret to someone, only to get burned for having done so. I once had a friend to whom I confided what I considered to be an intimate secret. In talking to a friend of my friend, I became painfully aware of the fact that this person, who was no friend of mine, knew every detail. Needless to say, I never confided in the so-called friend again and was, for a while, hesitant to confide in anyone.

Intimacy, then, is a foundation of love, but a foundation that develops slowly, through fits and starts, and is difficult to achieve. Moreover, once it starts to be attained, it may, paradoxically, start to go away because of the threat it poses. It poses a threat in terms not only of the dangers of self-disclosure but of the danger one starts to feel to one's existence as a separate, autonomous being. Few people want to be "consumed" by a relationship, yet people may start to feel as if they are being consumed when they get too close to another human being. The result is a balancing act between intimacy and autonomy, which goes on throughout the lives of most couples, a balancing act in which a completely stable equilibrium is often never achieved. But this in itself is not necessarily bad: The swinging back and forth of the intimacy pendulum provides some of the excitement that keeps many relationships alive.

Passion

The passion component of love involves a "state of intense longing for *union* with the other."[6] Passion is largely the expression of desires and needs – such as for self-esteem, nurturance, affiliation, dominance, submission, and sexual fulfillment. The strengths of these various needs vary across persons, situations, and kinds of loving relationship. For example, sexual fulfillment is likely to be a strong need in romantic relationships but not in filial ones. These needs manifest themselves through psychological and physiological arousal, which are often inseparable from each other.

Passion in love can tend to interweave itself with feelings of intimacy, and often they fuel each other. For example, intimacy in a relationship may be largely a function of the extent to which the relationship meets a person's need for passion. Conversely, passion may be aroused by intimacy. In some close relationships with members of the opposite sex, for example, the passion component develops almost immediately, and intimacy, only after a while. Passion may have drawn the individuals into the relationship in the first place, but intimacy helps sustain the closeness in the relationship. In other close relationships, however, passion, especially as it applies to physical attraction, develops only after intimacy. Two close friends of the opposite sex may find themselves eventually developing a physical attraction for each other once they have achieved a certain emotional intimacy.

Sometimes intimacy and passion work against each other. For example, in a relationship with a prostitute, a man may seek to maximize fulfillment of the need for passion while purposefully minimizing intimacy. An inverse relation between intimacy and passion can be a function of the person as well as of the situation: Some people find that the attainment of emotional closeness and intimacy actually interferes with sexual fulfillment, or that passionate involvement is detrimental to emotional intimacy. The point, quite simply, is that although the interaction between intimacy and passion will vary across people and across situations, these two components of love will almost certainly interact in close relationships in one way or another.

Most people, when they think of passion, view it as sexual – as the classic feeling of being "turned on." But any form of psychophysiological arousal can generate the experience of passion. For example, an individual with a high need for affiliation may experience passion toward an individual who provides him or her with a unique opportunity to affiliate. That person gives the needy person the desired sense of belonging.

These patterns of response have been established through years of observation and sometimes firsthand experience, which cannot be easily undone by a social worker or anyone else in a few months. Probably the strangest learning mechanism for the buildup of passionate response is the mechanism of *intermittent reinforcement*, the periodic, sometimes random rewarding of a particular response to a stimulus. If you try to accomplish something, and sometimes are rewarded for your efforts and sometimes not, you are being intermittently reinforced.

Oddly enough, intermittent reinforcement is even more powerful in continuing or sustaining a given pattern of behavior than is continuous reinforcement. You are more likely to lose interest in or desire for something, and to become bored, if you are always rewarded when you seek it than if you are sometimes rewarded, but sometimes not. Put another way, sometimes the fun is in wanting something rather than in getting it. And if you are never rewarded for a particular pattern of behavior, you are likely to give up on it ("extinguish it," as learning theorists would say), if only because of the total frustration you experience when you act in that particular way.

Passion thrives on the intermittent reinforcement that is usually most intense in the early stages of a relationship. When you want someone, sometimes you feel as if you are getting closer to him or her, and sometimes you feel you are not – an alternation that keeps the passion aroused. Thus, the little boy may, in seeking out his mother, feel for a while that he is making progress in getting her; but then he must come to terms with the fact that he can never have her in the way he wants. Those passionate feelings do not entirely disappear, however. Rather, they go into a latent state, waiting to be rekindled, usually years later, by a female peer.

The stimulus that rekindles the passion is similar to the stimulus of the past – the mother. And the pattern of intermittent reinforcement starts again, except that this time one has some hope of getting the object of desire. But if the getting or the keeping is too easy, and continuous reinforcement replaces the intermittent kind, the man may, ironically, lose interest in what he has been seeking. The same principles apply for women, but with respect to the father.

Decision and Commitment

The decision/commitment component of love consists of two aspects – one short-term and one long-term. The short-term aspect is the decision to love a certain other, whereas the long-term one is the commitment to maintain that love. These two aspects of the decision/commitment component of love do not necessarily occur together. The decision to love does not necessarily imply a commitment to that love. Oddly enough, the reverse is also possible, where there is a commitment to a relationship in which you did not make the decision, as in arranged marriages. Some people are committed to loving another without ever having admitted their love. Most often, however, a decision precedes the commitment. Indeed, the institution of marriage represents a legalization of the commitment to a decision to love another throughout life.

While the decision/commitment component of love may lack the "heat" or "charge" of intimacy and passion, loving relationships almost inevitably have their ups and downs, and during the downs, the decision/commitment component is what keeps a relationship together. This component can be essential for getting through hard times and for returning to better ones. In ignoring it or separating it from love, you may be missing exactly that component of a loving relationship that enables you to get through the hard times as well as the easy ones. Sometimes, you may have to trust your commitment to carry you through to the better times you hope are ahead.

The decision/commitment component of love interrelates to both intimacy and passion. For most people, it results from the combination of intimate involvement and passionate arousal; however, intimate involvement or passionate arousal can follow from commitment, as in certain arranged marriages or in close relationships in which you do not have a choice of partners. For example, you do not get to choose your mother, father, siblings, aunts, uncles, or cousins. In these close relationships, you may find that whatever intimacy or passion you experience results from your cognitive commitment to the relationship, rather than the other way around.

Love and commitment overlap, but you can have one without the other.[7] Harold Kelley has given as an example the Michelle Triola – Lee Marvin lawsuit, in which Triola sued the actor Marvin for "palimony." Although Triola and Marvin had lived together for some time, they had never been married. And, however they may have loved each other, permanent commitment was clearly not in Marvin's mind.

Commitment is the extent to which a person is likely to stick with something or someone and see it (or him or her) through to the finish. A person who is committed to something is expected to persist until the goal underlying the commitment is achieved. A problem for contemporary relationships is that two members of a couple may have different ideas about what it means to stick with someone to the end or to the realization of a goal. These differences, moreover, may never be articulated. One person, for example, may see the "end" as that point where the relationship is no longer working, whereas the other may see the end as the ending of one of the couple's lives. In a time of changing values and notions of commitment, it is becoming increasingly common for partners to find themselves in disagreement about the exact nature and duration of their commitment to each other. When marital commitments were always and automatically assumed to be for life, divorce was clearly frowned upon. Today, divorce in many parts of the world is clearly more acceptable than it was even thirty years ago, in part because many people have different ideas about how durable and lasting the marital commitment need be. People are also more aware of how much individuals can change, so that the person one comes to be with seems not to be, in many respects, the person to whom one originally made a commitment.

Difficulties deriving from mismatches between notions of commitment cannot always be worked out by discussing mutual definitions of it, because these definitions may change over time and differently for the two members of a couple. Both partners may intend a lifelong commitment at the time of marriage, for example; but one of them may have a change of mind – or of heart – over time. Moreover, it is important to distinguish between commitment to a person and commitment to a relationship. While two people may both be committed to each other, one may see the commitment as extending to the person and to a relationship with that person, but not necessarily to the type of relationship the couple has had up to a certain point. This person may wish to alter the kind of relationship the couple has. For example, one may be committed to one's husband and to having a relationship with that husband, but not to the kind of submissive role one has taken in the past with respect to him.

PROPERTIES OF THE COMPONENTS OF LOVE

The three components of love have different properties (see Table 1.1). For example, intimacy and commitment seem to be relatively stable in close relationships, whereas passion tends to be relatively unstable and

Table 1.1. *Properties of the triangle*

Properties	Intimacy	Passion	Decision/commitment
Stability	Moderately high	Low	Moderately high
Conscious controllability	Moderate	Low	High
Experiential salience	Variable	High	Variable
Typical importance in short-term relationships	Moderate	High	Low
Typical importance in long-term relationships	High	Moderate	High
Commonality across loving relationships	High	Low	Moderate
Psychophysiological involvement	Moderate	High	Low
Susceptibility to conscious awareness	Moderately low	High	Moderately high

can fluctuate unpredictably. You have some degree of conscious control over your feelings of intimacy (if you are aware of them), a high degree of control over the commitment of the decision/commitment component that you invest in the relationship (again, if we assume awareness), but little control over the amount of passionate arousal you experience as a result of being with or even looking at another person. You are usually aware and conscious of passion, but you are less likely to be fully aware of intimacy and commitment. Sometimes you experience warm feelings of intimacy without being aware of them or able to label them. Similarly, you are often not certain of how committed you are to a relationship until people or events intervene to challenge that commitment.

The importance of each of the three components of love varies, on average, according to whether a loving relationship is short-term or long-term. In short-term involvements, and especially romantic ones, passion tends to play a large part, whereas intimacy may play only a moderate part, and decision/commitment may play hardly any part at all. In contrast, in a long-term close relationship, intimacy and decision/commitment typically must play relatively large parts.

In such a relationship, passion typically plays only a moderate part, and its role may decline somewhat over time. The three components of love also differ in their presence in various loving relationships. Intimacy appears to be at the core of many loving relationships, whether that relationship is with parent, sibling, lover, or close friend. Passion tends to be limited to certain kinds of loving relationships, especially romantic ones, whereas decision/commitment can be highly variable across different loving relationships. For example, commitment tends to be high in love for one's children, but relatively low in love for friends who come and go throughout the span of a life.

The three components also differ in the amount of psychophysiological arousal they offer. Passion is highly dependent on psychophysiological arousal, whereas decision/commitment appears to involve relatively little psychophysiological response. Intimacy involves an intermediate amount of psychophysiological arousal.

In sum, the three components of love have somewhat different properties, which tend to highlight some of the ways they function in the experiences of love as they occur in various close relationships. These three components generate seven different kinds of love, as discussed in Chapter 2.

2
Seven Kinds of Love

There may be just three main components of love but, in combination, they produce seven different kinds of love. These kinds of love differ in how many of the components and in which of the components of love they comprise.[1] A summary of the seven different kinds of love is shown in Table 2.1.

KINDS OF LOVE

Liking (Solely Intimacy)

Joe was intensely jealous. After seven months, he had thought he and Stephanie were "a couple." But Stephanie seemed to be spending almost as much time with Alex as she was spending with Joe. Joe was afraid she was two-timing him. Finally, he confronted her.

"I just can't stand this any more."

"Huh? What can't you stand?"

"Your relationship with Alex. If you prefer him to me, that's fine. Just say the word, and I'll be on my way. But you seem to want us both, and I just won't stand for it any longer."

"I don't know what you're talking about. Alex is no competition for you – none at all. What in the world makes you think he is?"

"But you're spending as much time with him as you are with me, not to mention what you may be doing with that time."

Table 2.1. *Taxonomy of kinds of love*

Kind of love	Intimacy	Passion	Decision/commitment
Nonlove	−	−	−
Liking	+	−	−
Infatuated love	−	+	−
Empty love	−	−	+
Romantic love	+	+	−
Companionate love	+	−	+
Fatuous love	−	+	+
Consummate love	+	+	+

Note: + = component present; − = component absent. These kinds of love represent idealized cases based on the triangular theory. Most loving relationships will fit between categories, because the components of love occur in varying degrees, rather than being simply present or absent.

"Joe, you're off, you're way off. Alex is a good friend. I do like his company. I like doing things with him. I like talking to him. But I don't love him, and I never will. I don't plan to spend my life with him. He's a friend, and nothing more, but nothing less either."

"Oh, I see."

But Joe didn't really see that Stephanie's relationship with Alex was a friendship, and nothing more. He was still jealous, his words notwithstanding.

Liking results when you experience only the intimacy component of love without passion or decision/commitment. The term *liking* is used here in a nontrivial sense, to describe not merely the feelings you have toward casual acquaintances and passers-by, but rather the set of feelings you experience in relationships that can truly be characterized as friendships. You feel closeness, bondedness, and warmth toward the other, without feelings of intense passion or long-term commitment. Stated another way, you feel emotionally close to the friend, but the friend does not arouse your passion or make you feel that you want to spend the rest of your life with him or her.

It is possible for friendships to have elements of passionate arousal or long-term commitment, but such friendships go beyond mere liking. You can use the absence test to distinguish mere liking from love that goes beyond liking. If a typical friend whom you like goes away, even for an extended period of time, you may miss him or her, but you probably will not dwell on the loss. You can pick up the friendship some years later, often in a different form, without even having thought much about the friendship during the intervening years. When a close relationship goes beyond liking, however, you actively miss the other person and tend to dwell on or be preoccupied with his or her absence. The absence has a substantial and fairly long-term effect on your life. When the absence of the other arouses strong feelings of intimacy, passion, or commitment, the relationship has gone beyond liking.

Infatuated Love (Solely Passion)

Tom met Lisa at work. One look at her was enough to change his life: He fell madly in love with her. Instead of concentrating on his work, he would think about Lisa. She was aware of his feelings, but did not much care for Tom. When he tried to start a conversation with her, she moved on as quickly as possible.

Tom's staring and his awkwardness in talking to her made Lisa feel uncomfortable. He, on the other hand, could think of little else besides Lisa, and his work began to suffer as the time he should have been devoting to it went instead to thinking about Lisa. He was a man obsessed. The obsession might have gone on indefinitely, but Lisa moved away. Tom never saw Lisa again and, after several unanswered love letters, he finally gave up on her.

Tom's "love at first sight" is infatuated love or, simply, infatuation. It results from the experiencing of passionate arousal without the intimacy and decision/commitment components of love. Infatuation is usually obvious, although it tends to be somewhat easier for others to spot than for the person who is experiencing it. An infatuation can arise almost instantaneously and dissipate as quickly. Infatuations generally come with a high degree of psychophysiological arousal and bodily symptoms such as increased heartbeat or even palpitations of the heart, increased hormonal secretions, and erection of genitals (penis or clitoris). They will probably cause no problem unless an individual believes infatuation to be more than it is.

Empty Love (Solely Decision/Commitment)

John and Mary had been married for twenty years. For fifteen of them, Mary had been thinking about getting a divorce, but could never get herself to go through with it. Because she did not work outside the home, she was afraid she would be unable to make a living; besides, life alone might be worse than with John. And life with John was not bad. Basically, he left her alone. He was almost never home; when he was, he pretty much stuck to doing his work. Whatever passion they might once have had was long since gone. Mary had long felt that John had found other women, and even the little intimacy they had once had vanished. At this point, they hardly ever even talked. Mary often wondered whether John would leave, and sometimes wished he would. But he seemed content to have her wash his clothes, prepare his meals, keep house, and do all the things that she had long ago been taught a wife should do. Mary often felt that her life would be completely empty were it not for her children.

Mary's kind of love emanates from the decision that you love another and are committed to that love even without having the intimacy or the passion associated with some loves. It is the love sometimes found in stagnant relationships that have been going on for years but that have lost both their original mutual emotional involvement and physical attraction. Unless the commitment to the love is very strong, such love can be close to none at all. Although in our society we see empty love generally as the final or near final stage of a long-term relationship, in other societies empty love may be the first stage of a long-term relationship. In societies where marriages are arranged, the marital partners start with the commitment to love each other, or to try to do so, and not much more. Here, *empty* denotes a relationship that may come to be filled with passion and intimacy, and thus marks a beginning rather than an end.

Romantic Love (Intimacy plus Passion)

Susan and Ralph met in their junior year of college. Their relationship started off as a good friendship, but rapidly turned into a deeply involved romantic love affair. They spent as much time together as possible, and enjoyed practically every minute of it. But Susan and Ralph were not ready to commit themselves permanently to the relationship: Both felt they were too young to make any long-term decisions and that, until they at least knew where they would go after college, it was impossible to tell even how much they could be together. Ralph was admitted to graduate study in Los Angeles and decided to go there. Susan, an engineer, had applied to a program in Los Angeles and was accepted, but without financial aid. She was also accepted by a program in Boston with a large fellowship. The difference in financial packages left her with little choice but to go to Boston. When she went out East, neither she nor Ralph had much confidence that their relationship would survive the distance; after a year of occasional commutes and not so occasional strains, it ended.

Ralph and Susan's relationship combines the intimacy and passion components of love. It is liking with an added element: namely, the arousal brought about by physical attraction. In this type of love, the man and woman are not only drawn physically to each other but are also bonded emotionally. This is the view of romantic love found in classic works of literature, such as *Romeo and Juliet*.

Companionate Love (Intimacy plus Commitment)

In their twenty years of marriage, Sam and Sara had been through some rough times. They had seen many of their friends through divorces, Sam through several jobs, and Sara through a nearly fatal illness. Both had friends, but there was no doubt in either of their minds that they were each other's best friend. They knew they could count on each other. Neither Sam nor Sara felt any great passion in their relationship, but they had never sought out others, because they both believed they had what mattered most to them: the ability to say or do anything they might want without fear of attack or reprisal. Although they each knew there were probably limits to their regard for each other, they had never sought to test these limits, because they were happy to live within them.

Sam and Sara's kind of love evolves from a combination of the intimacy and decision/commitment components of love. It is essentially a long-term, committed friendship, the kind that frequently occurs in marriages in which physical attraction (a major source of passion) has waned.

Fatuous Love (Passion plus Commitment)

When Tim and Diana met at a resort in the Bahamas, they were both on the rebound. Tim's fiancée had abruptly broken off their engagement and essentially eloped with the man who had been Tim's close colleague. Moreover, Tim had just lost his job. Diana was recently divorced, the victim of the "other woman." Each felt desperate for love, and when they met each other, they immediately saw themselves as a perfect match. Indeed, it was as though someone had watched over them, seen their plight, and brought them together in their time of need. The manager of the resort, always on the lookout for vacation romances as good publicity, offered to marry them at the resort and to throw a lavish reception at no charge, other than cooperation in promotional materials. After thinking it over, Tim and Diana agreed. They knew they were right for each other, and because neither was particularly well off at the moment, the possibility of a free wedding was appealing.

Regrettably, the marriage proved to be a disaster once Tim and Diana returned from their vacation. Although he was great fun to be with, Tim had never been one for taking employment seriously, whereas Diana expected him to get a job and support her. Tim, in turn, was shocked to learn that Diana did not expect to work, thus disappointing his expectations of receiving at least some financial support from her in order to further his aspiration to become a poet.

Fatuous love, as in the case of Tim and Diana, results from the combination of passion and decision/commitment without intimacy, which takes time to develop. It is the kind of love we sometimes associate with Hollywood or with other whirlwind courtships, in which a couple meets one day, gets engaged soon thereafter, and marries almost immediately. This love is fatuous in the sense that the partners commit

themselves to one another on the basis of passion without the stabiliz-
ing element of intimate involvement. Because passion can develop almost instantaneously, and intimacy cannot, relationships based on
fatuous love are not likely to last.

Consummate Love (Intimacy
plus Passion plus Commitment)

Harry and Edith seemed to all their friends to be the perfect couple.
What made them distinctive from many such "perfect couples" is that
they pretty much fulfilled the notion. They felt close to each other, they
continued to have great sex after fifteen years, and they could not imagine themselves happy over the long term with anyone else. They had
weathered their few storms, and each was delighted with the relationship and with each other.

Consummate, or complete, love like Edith and Harry's results from
the combination of the three components in equal measure. It is a love
toward which many of us strive, especially in romantic relationships.
Attaining consummate love is analogous, in at least one respect, to
meeting your goal in a weight-reduction program: Reaching your ideal
weight is often easier than maintaining it. Attaining consummate love
is no guarantee that it will last; one may become aware of the loss only
after it is far gone. Consummate love, like other things of value, must
be guarded carefully.

I do not believe that all aspects of consummate love are necessarily
difficult either to develop or to maintain. For example, love for one's
children often carries with it the deep emotional involvement of the intimacy component, the satisfaction of motivational needs (such as nurturance, self-esteem, self-actualization) of the passion component, and
the firm commitment of the decision/commitment component. For
many but not all parents, formation and maintenance of this love is no
problem. Perhaps the bonding between parents and children at birth
renders this love relatively easier to maintain, or perhaps evolutionary
forces are at work to ensure that parent–child bonding survives at least
those formative years in which the child must depend heavily on the
parent's love and support. Whichever of these possibilities holds (and
it may be more than one), whether consummate love is easy or hard to

form and maintain depends on the relationship and on how supportive the situation is of the relationship.

INFATUATION VERSUS ROMANTIC LOVE

When all is said and done, one of the most important problems we all
face is that of distinguishing romantic love, or the experience of being
"in love," with passionate love, or mere "infatuation." Research suggests that people perceive being in love, but not infatuation, as a genuine type of love.[2] How can one tell the difference?

A set of signs of true romantic love has been proposed by a noted
Italian investigator of love, Francesco Alberoni.[3] These signs distinguish being in love from infatuation. The more of them you feel, the
more in love you are likely to be. Some of the main signs include the
feeling that you have met the person who is truly right for you; the feeling that, at some level, you have been reborn; the feeling that material
possessions just no longer matter as much to you; the feeling of wanting to share all with your beloved; and the feeling that you would like
to fuse your spirit with that of the loved one. Of course, these feelings
can be viewed only subjectively and, in themselves, may even be mis-
leading.

These feelings represent the strong sense of intimacy and passion you
feel toward your partner and, perhaps at the moment, a feeling of commitment as well, although not necessarily to an indefinite future (which
is why consummate love takes time to grow). The intimacy and passion that constitute your triangle and perhaps that of your lover are
only two of the triangles that appear in any loving relationship. There
are other triangles as well, as discussed in Chapter 3.

3

Many Different
Triangles of Love

The Love Triangles

We can have many different triangles of love for a given relationship. The triangles have in common three vertices: intimacy, passion, and commitment. They differ in size (amount of love), in shape (balance of love), in whether they represent what you have (the real relationship) or what you wish you had (the ideal relationship), and in whether they represent your feelings or your actions. Moreover, each partner has a different set of triangles. What are all these different triangles, and how do they come about?

THE GEOMETRY OF THE LOVE TRIANGLE

Allen and Wendy knew they loved each other. They also knew they had a problem. For Allen, true love was based on physical passion. After a series of unsatisfactory relationships, he had come to the conclusion that any difficulty could be resolved if a couple was good in bed. For Wendy, closeness had to come first. She just couldn't go to bed with Allen if they were having an argument or feeling distant from each other. But her attitude frustrated Allen, because he believed that there was scarcely a problem that a couple couldn't work out in bed, if only given the chance. At the same time, Wendy felt frustrated with Allen: Solutions to problems had to come before going to bed; they couldn't come out of going to bed, because then they were not really solutions at all, but rather avoidance of the problems. Eventually, Allen and

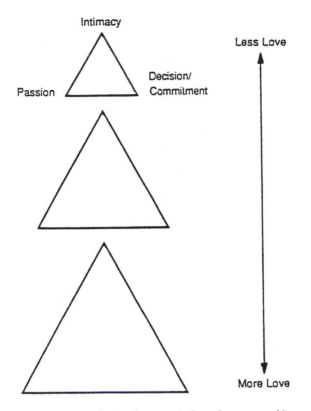

Figure 3.1. Area of triangle as an index of amount of love.

Wendy split up, unable to resolve this fundamental difference between them.

Love triangles can have different shapes. It is clear that Allen and Wendy had different ideas of what the shape of the love triangle should be. The geometry of the love triangle depends on two factors: amount of love and balance of love.

Amount of Love: Area of the Triangle

Figure 3.1 shows three triangles differing only in area. These differences in area represent differences in amounts of love experienced in three hypothetical relationships: The larger the triangle, the greater the

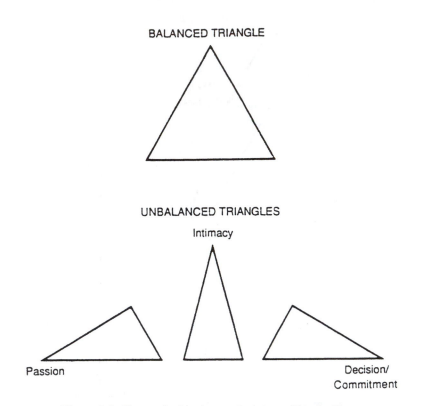

Figure 3.2. Shape of triangle as a function of kind of love.

amount of experienced love. It is actually possible to specify coordinates for the three components of love, with higher absolute values of coordinates representing greater amounts of each of the three components of love.

Balance of Love: Shape of the Triangle

Figure 3.2 shows four distinct triangles that are dissimilar in shape. The triangle at the top has three equal sides, and represents balanced love, in which all three components of love are roughly equally matched. The second triangle, with no two sides of equal length, represents a relationship in which passion is emphasized over the other components of love. In this relationship, physical attraction is likely to play a larger part than do intimacy and decision/commitment. The third triangle, with two sides equal in length, represents a relationship in which intimacy plays a large part and passion and decision/commitment play smaller parts. This triangle represents a relationship in which the two lovers are good friends and close to each other, but the physical aspects and commitment to the future are marginal. The fourth triangle represents a relationship in which the decision/commitment component rules over intimacy and passion. This triangle represents a highly committed relationship in which intimacy and physical attraction have waned or were never present in the first place. Of course, other possibilities exist as well, such as a triangle in which two components are about equal, and a third one is lower or higher in value.

By varying both the area and the shape of the triangle of love, one can represent a wide variety of relationships and, particularly, the course of a close relationship over time. The triangle is, of course, only a gross representation of the subtleties of love in a relationship. As mentioned earlier, the intimacy component in a loving relationship is not a single feeling but rather a union of many different feelings. Similarly, many different sources of passion may enter into love in a close relationship, and a variety of conditions in the decision/commitment component yield the decision to love someone and the decision to remain committed to that love. Hence, a detailed diagnosis of the state of a relationship necessitates going beyond looking only at the area and the shape of the triangle. Moreover, there is much more than love to making a relationship work. For example, such factors as financial security, views on how to bring up children, possible external supports in raising children, and parental involvement can contribute to making or breaking a relationship. For some, friendship may be all they are looking for, but other couples may be frustrated by their inability to attain anything more.

Richard and Martha, for example, recently split up. For years, each was the other's best friend. They got along beautifully, never seemed to fight, and did lots of things together. They were the couple everyone was betting on, the one people were sure would not split up. After they did split up, I talked to both of them. Martha, the one who decided to leave, still describes Richard as her best friend. But her frustration with the relationship, she told me, was that she and Richard were "more like roommates than lovers." She wanted a friend, but she also wanted more, and felt that no matter how she tried, she couldn't get it from Richard. The relationship was warm, she said, but never, ever hot. There was no passion between them. Richard's characterization of the relationship was similar to Martha's. But he was in great pain over her, to him, unexpected and unjustified decision to leave. He believed they had what love is in a long-term relationship: Sure, there may be intense passion early on, but, according to Richard, that passion is quickly replaced by friendship. Thus, each member of the couple defined differently what it means to love in a long-term relationship – a difference Martha found irreconcilable.

Relationships involving little more than passion are by no means rare. Sometimes the passion is requited, and it can happen within, as well as outside of, a marriage.

Jason and Bernadette are a case in point. Married for three years, they fight constantly and cheat in their fights, hitting "below the belt" with great regularity. (Ironically, Jason is a consultant whose job it is to create harmony within large organizations.) If Jason and Bernadette like each other, they hide it well from the outside world and even from one another. What holds them together? "Sex," Jason says, "the best sex I've ever had by far, and I've had a lot of it." According to Jason, he and Bernadette even fight when they make love, and he likes it that way. For him, anyway, it adds to the excitement. "Romance," says Bernadette. "We don't get along, but we're madly in love with each other, and it's been that way for three years. It was even that way when we were going out. We've never gotten along, but it's like magnetism: We're the opposite poles that attract." Whether they are aware of it or not, Jason and Bernadette are strongly committed to each other.

Many couples stay together because of a conscious commitment – sometimes a direct one with respect to each other, but other times an indirect one. In the latter case, the partners may be committed actually to the institution of marriage, to keeping an intact family for the sake of the children, to keeping financial solvency, or to any of a number of other things. There are, for example, many couples like Jerry and Susan.

Susan describes herself as feeling nothing at all for Jerry. Once she loved him, but no more. She has entertained the idea of leaving, but in all likelihood never will. Why does she stay? "For the kids," she says (they have two), "and because I have no money and no marketable skills. I could try to slug it out in court, but I'd lose; he's as much as told me that if I ever leave him I won't get a dime. I believe him. I just can't take the chance. Maybe I'd do it if I were the only one involved, but I'm not. I can't risk my kids." For Susan, what is left is commitment to a life she feels she can have only if she stays with Jerry.

The sizes and shapes of triangles may be translated into the day-to-day events that shape and are shaped by relationships. Relationships where people are differentially involved – different sizes of triangles – often fail because the less involved partner feels as if he or she cannot provide what the more involved partner wants, whereas the more involved partner feels as if the less-involved partner is always holding back and preventing the relationship from realizing its full potential.

If each partner has a triangle of a different shape, the result can be equally devastating. If one partner is frustrated owing to lack of intimacy, and the other owing to lack of passion, it is unlikely there will be any meeting of the minds – or of anything else – when the couple attempts to make the relationship work. Each wants what the other does not have to offer, and the couple is likely to go around and around, trying to make work a relationship that is failing because of the different "love triangles" each partner desires.

THE OTHER TRIANGLES OF LOVE

Gene, at the age of thirty-six, was reasonably happy and eager to get married. But although he had met several women over the years, he did not feel that any of them were quite right for him. He viewed himself as having high standards, and none of the women he had met could quite measure up to them. Gene could not see himself entering into a permanent relationship with a woman he felt was not what he really wanted. And none of the women he had met were really what he wanted. Early on in some of his relationships, he had thought he had found what he was looking for, only to become disappointed once he got to know the women better. Discouraged, he wondered whether he would ever find the woman of his dreams. Friends suggested that he set more reasonable standards, but he did not view his standards as unreasonable. A marriage that represented a compromise could hardly be a marriage at all for him, because he would always wonder whether waiting just a little bit longer might not find him the woman he had always been looking for.

Recall that love involves not just a single triangle but, rather, a great number of triangles. The main kinds of triangles are real versus ideal, self-perceived versus other-perceived, and feelings versus actions. Consider each of these kinds of triangles.

Real versus Ideal Triangles

There is, in a close relationship, not only the triangle representing your love for the other but also one representing an ideal other in that relationship. This ideal may be based, in part, on experience in previous relationships of the same kind and, in part, on expectations of what the close relationship can be.[1] Expectations of a relationship's potential may or may not be grounded in reality.

Dahlia's relationship with her husband, Layton, is not much different from the relationship most of her friends have with their husbands. Of this fact, Dahlia is sure from innumerable coffee-klatch and bridge-club conversations. The difference between Dahlia and her friends, though, is one of expectations – of ideals. Dahlia's friends don't seem to expect much, and they are more or less getting what they expect. Dahlia has had and continues to have dreams of great closeness – of cherished intimacy and sharing and support. These things Dahlia does not have. Her "real triangle" is about the same as that of her friends. Her ideal triangle, however, seeks more intimacy from her relationship. Because she is not getting it, she experiences a sense of dissatisfaction her friends do not experience.

Figure 3.3 represents four of the possible relations between real and ideal triangles. The first panel shows real and ideal triangles as the same: In other words, the actual relationship corresponds essentially perfectly to the ideal for that relationship. The second panel shows underinvolvement: The person's triangle in the actual relationship shows

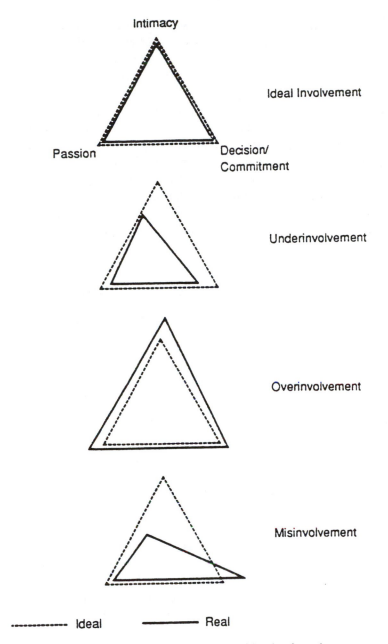

Figure 3.3. Relations between real and ideal levels of involvement.

lower levels of the three components than the person ideally would like. The third panel shows overinvolvement: Levels of the three components are greater than one would like. The fourth triangle shows misinvolvement: Here levels of intimacy and passion are less than what one ideally might desire, but the level of decision/commitment is greater than that desired. Whereas the second and third triangles involve mismatches primarily in area, the fourth triangle involves mismatch primarily in shape. Of course, it is possible to have mismatches in both area and shape or in neither, as in the first triangle.

The overlapping area between the real and the ideal triangles is associated with satisfaction in close relationships., whereas the nonoverlapping area between the two triangles is associated with dissatisfaction. In other words, once again, you are happier when the level of involvement is close to what you want, neither more nor less.

Self-Perceived versus Other-Perceived Triangles

It is also possible to distinguish between self-perceived (the way you see things) and other-perceived (the way your partner sees things) triangles. In a loving relationship, you have a triangle that represents your love for the other person. However, there is no guarantee that this triangle of the way you feel will be experienced by the other in the same way it is experienced by you. Because your partner in a loving relationship may not perceive your level of the three components of love in the same way you perceive your involvement, there can be discrepancies between one triangle as experienced by the self and as experienced by the other. Figure 3.4 shows two possible levels of discrepancy – one minor and one major – between self- and other-perceived triangles.

Lennart views himself as caring, giving, concerned, and responsible. It is hard to imagine a better and more thoughtful husband. Liv is lucky to have a husband like him. Liv feels rather differently. Lennart's specialty, she believes, is in projecting images. At one time, those images played loud and clear on her picture screen. Now she realizes that what she was seeing were indeed movies. Lennart is nothing like the images he projects. Unfortunately, he does not realize this fact himself. At some level, he believes the movie script he has created. So his self-projected triangle looks nothing like the one Liv perceives him as truly offering.

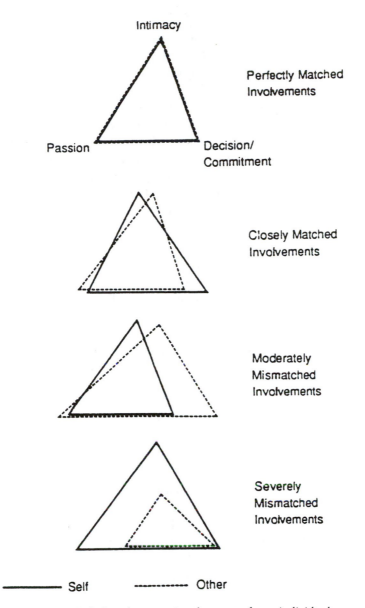

Figure 3.4. Relations between involvement of two individuals in a relationship.

Feelings versus Action Triangles

Craig had assured Lucy that she was everything to him – that his life would mean nothing without her. But his actions did not clearly reflect his words. At first, she was very pleased with his assurances. She wanted a man who put her as his top priority in his life. But over time, the assurances began to wear thin: Although Craig said that Lucy was the most important thing in his life, she did not feel that he acted that way. He traveled a great deal, and when he was around, he always seemed to have things to do that took precedence over Lucy. Craig and Lucy talked about her perception, and he assured her that he understood why she would feel as she did – but also that she was misconstruing his actions, because it was she who came first. At the same time, though, he did have other responsibilities and could not very well just let them be unfulfilled. Eventually, Lucy decided to leave the relationship: Unable to reconcile Craig's actions with his words, she decided that actions speak louder than words.

The case of Lucy and Craig shows how feelings and actions can diverge. There can be any number of sources of the discrepancy between the way one person feels toward another and the way the other perceives that feeling. But almost certainly one of the most powerful sources is the failure to express one's love fully in action. It is one thing to feel a certain way but another thing altogether to express these feelings, and often the feelings fail to be communicated because of one's inability or unwillingness to show one's feelings of love.

Another source of discrepancy is the fact that certain actions performed by a person as demonstrating love may not be perceived by the other as such, or may go unnoticed altogether. This discrepancy may be due to different backgrounds or upbringings, through which individuals come to understand behavior to mean certain things. This situation is most evident in couples who come from different cultural or religious backgrounds, where notions of what is involved in a close relationship may differ.

When people come from different cultures, an action viewed by one individual as loving may be seen by the other as cold or meaningless. Consider, for example, physical affection. For some people, signs of physical affection – holding, touching, caressing, stroking – are crucial ingredients of romantic love; for others, they are not. The importance of overt physical affection also may differ across cultures.

Each of the three components of love is expressed through particular actions. For example, you might express intimacy by communicating inner feelings; promoting the other's well-being; sharing your possessions, time, and self; expressing empathy for the other; and offering emotional and material support to the other. Some ways of expressing passion include kissing, hugging, gazing, touching, and making love. Some ways of expressing decision/commitment include pledging fidelity, staying in a relationship through hard times, engagement, and marriage. Of course, the actions that express a particular component of love can differ somewhat from one person to another, from one relationship to another, and from one situation to another.

Nevertheless, it is important to consider love as it is expressed through action, through concrete signs of love such as planning a surprise vacation, buying flowers or candy, making instead of buying a card, calling to say hello at an unexpected time, or whatever. Action has many different effects on a relationship. What are some of these effects?

First, actions can affect the level of the three components. One's feelings and thoughts can be affected by one's actions just as one's actions can be affected by one's feelings and thoughts.[2] In other words, the way people act shapes the way they feel and think, possibly as much as the way they feel and think shapes the way they act.

Second, certain actions lead to other actions. In other words, acting in certain ways tends to produce acting in related ways and, thus, to build up a network of actions. Expressing your love through action can lead to further expression of this love through action, whereas failure of self-expression can lead to further failure of this kind.

Third, the way you act is likely to affect the way the other feels and thinks about you. In other words, your actions can be expected to have an effect on the other's triangle of love for you.

Fourth, and finally, your actions will almost inevitably have an effect on the other's actions, thereby leading to a mutually reinforcing series of paired action sequences. What happens over time as these paired action sequences evolve?

HOW THE TRIANGLES OF LOVE
DEVELOP OVER TIME

Each of the three components of love has a different course, and the changes in each over time almost inevitably result in changes in the nature of a loving relationship.

Intimacy

Bill and Brenda had what for both of them was an ideal courtship. They shared the same interests and values and felt they could confide in each other. When they married, they felt they had every reason to expect a successful marriage. And it wasn't bad. But as time went on, they had less and less to say to each other, and sometimes found themselves manufacturing small talk to keep themselves occupied. Bill worked hard, but didn't believe in bringing his work home with him and so didn't talk to Brenda about it. Brenda was involved in running a shelter for abused women, but Bill didn't seem very interested in hearing about what Brenda did there. Their sexual relationship continued to be good, but they felt themselves drifting away from each other. It wasn't any one thing – just a slow, seemingly inexorable drift. What had started as an intimate relationship became rather distant, and eventually Brenda remarked that she felt that they were living in parallel rather than together. At that point, they sought marital counseling, which succeeded in bringing them back together as they realized that their lack of communication and mutual support had become essentially a bad habit, but one that could be broken with effort on both their parts.

The course of the intimacy component of love is based on contemporary theories of emotion in close relationships.[3] According to these theories, emotion in close relationships is experienced only as the result of interruption of common and well-rehearsed interactions between partners – what might be referred to as *scripts*. In other words, if an expected action is performed, it will not cause you to feel any particular unexpected emotion; but if your partner fails to perform an expected action or performs an unexpected action, you are most likely to feel some unexpected emotion in respect to it.

As two people get to know each other, they form increasing numbers of scripts. Early in a relationship, each person will be highly uncertain about what the other will feel, say, or do, because neither has yet become able to predict the other. In general, there will be frequent interruptions and disruptions of the relationship as the two people get to know each other. As time goes on, the frequency of interruptions is likely to decrease, because the partners are getting to know each other better, becoming more predictable to each other, and becoming dependent on each other for expected behavior. As the interruption decreases, so will the experienced emotion. Eventually a partner may experience little or no emotion at all.

The decrease in experienced intimacy in a close relationship, especially a romantic one, has both a positive and a negative side. The positive side is that the decrease in experienced intimacy is the result of an increase in interpersonal bonding: In other words, it results from the relationship's becoming closer. The partners are so connected with each other that the one doesn't recognize the other is there, just as the air we breathe can be taken for granted, despite its necessity to life. Thus, the relationship might be viewed as having a large amount of hidden intimacy. The negative side is that the lack of observable intimacy often makes it difficult to distinguish the close relationship from no relationship at all.

This situation is represented in Figure 3.5, which shows both hidden and experienced levels of intimacy as a function of the time course of the relationship. The failed or failing relationship will differ from the successful relationship in terms primarily of the hidden intimacy rather than of the experienced or observable intimacy.

Fortunately, there are ways of distinguishing a live relationship from one that is dying or dead. The most obvious way is to generate some interruption (unpredicted action or change in behavior) in order to activate intimacy. For example, the lover's going away, even for a brief period, can help you ascertain how much feeling you still have for him or her. Or, changing established routines, as on a joint vacation, can be useful in assessing the state of intimacy in a relationship.

Sometimes it is only through extreme intervention, whether intentional or unintentional, that one learns how much intimacy one has or has had in a relationship. For example, when one partner becomes seriously ill, the well partner is often surprised by his or her intense concern

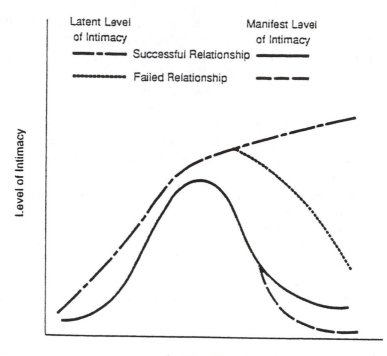

Figure 3.5. The course of intimacy as a function of duration of relationship.

and distress. Even partners who have pretty much taken their relationship for granted may come to realize just how important the partner's well-being is to them. The intimacy was there, even if the couple was unaware of it. Similarly, couples who argue and never seem to get along can have considerable intimacy invested in the relationship, whatever the nature of that intimacy may be.[4] According to this view of the course of intimacy in close relationships, it is essential that couples experience minor interruptions so that they can recapture awareness of their intimate involvement before they create such a major interruption as divorce.

Passion

When Rick met Sally, he felt passionate love for the first time. He had had other relationships and a string of casual affairs, but the relationship with Sally was different: He had never before felt truly passionate toward and engrossed by a woman. Sally, in turn, viewed the relationship as her salvation. She had just finished the second of two disastrous relationships, and this one was as different as could be. Rick and Sally saw each other every day and made love every time they got together. Over time, the relationship continued to be rewarding, but both of them felt the passion dwindling. And they both worried: What happened to the passion they had felt toward each other? Where had it gone, and how could it be restored?

However much they tried, it wouldn't come back, and they felt a keen disappointment at the loss of what had once seemed so valuable to them. The course run by the passion component in close relationships is different from that of the intimacy component. The view presented here, shown in Figure 3.6, is based on what is called an opponent-process theory of acquired motivation.[5]

Experienced motivation (wanting or craving) for a person or an object is a function of two underlying opponent processes: The first, positive process, is quick to develop but also quick to fade; the second, negative or opponent process, is slow to develop and also slow to fade. The result of the two processes working in conjunction is a motivational course somewhat like that depicted in Figure 3.6.

The passion component appears to draw heavily on psychological and bodily arousal. Moreover, its course closely resembles that predicted by opponent-process theory. Thus, this theory provides a good description of the time course of the passion component, or at least its motivational aspects.

According to the theory as applied to love, you can experience a surge in passion almost immediately upon meeting another person to whom you are attracted, whether physically or otherwise. This passionate arousal increases quickly but also peaks fairly rapidly.

At the peak of arousal, a negative force begins to work in opposition to the passion. This force is important to a person's equilibrium, because it can help prevent the person from becoming hopelessly addicted, either to substances or to people. In love, it sometimes prevents passion from getting out of kilter (although not always, as crimes of passion illustrate). At the peak of arousal, the passion you experience begins to decrease; and under the influence of the negative force, you

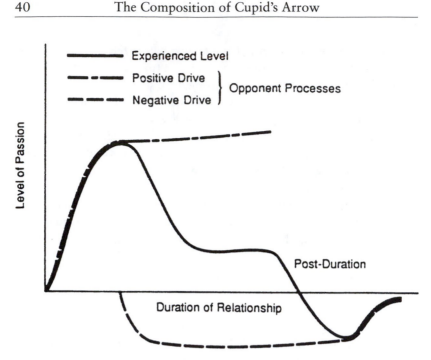

Figure 3.6. The course of passion as a function of duration of relationship.

will gradually reach a more or less stable state of *habituation* of feeling in respect to the person or the object.

Now both the positive and the negative (opponent) forces are in equilibrium. Should you lose the person (or the object), you do not merely go back to baseline – that is, the null level of passionate arousal you felt before encountering the person or object. Rather, you are likely to sink into depression, remorse, and extreme discomfort. This slide results from the loss of the positive passionate force (the person or object is gone) coupled with the continuance of the negative force (the effects of the absence continue to be felt). It is only gradually that the effects of the negative force, which is slow to disappear, begin to moderate and you eventually return to the state where you originally started.

It is useful to think of the motivational model in terms of an addiction. Indeed, the similarity of the passion component of love to the motivational aspect of an addiction has led some investigators to refer to love as an addiction.[6]

With addictive substances such as drugs, cigarettes, or coffee, one initially has no particular motivation toward or need for the addictive substance. When one starts to use the addictive substance, one feels a "high" as a result and is then likely to use more of the substance. With increased use, however, one starts to habituate: A given amount of the substance no longer has the same effect nor does it produce the same high it once did. Eventually one is so habituated as to need to continue the use of the substance merely to prevent withdrawal, with its resulting symptoms of depression, irritability, and craving for the substance. Should one cease use of the substance, there will be a difficult withdrawal period in which one experiences a variety of unpleasant psychological and somatic symptoms. After the withdrawal period has ended, one eventually returns to one's normal state. With regard to passion in relationships, many people find that the intense thrill of sex experienced at the beginning of a relationship moderates and transforms itself over time, although not necessarily into something less satisfying.

Decision and Commitment

Jeanne and Jim were nothing if not committed to each other: Nothing took priority over their relationship. They married after knowing each other for four years. Their marriage had the usual up-and-down swings, with some rocky times because Jim's job required frequent moves to enable him to climb the corporate ladder. But they got through it all. When Jim turned sixty, they decided they were ready for their second honeymoon. While on the honeymoon, they realized that even when they had married, they had not realized just how committed they could be to each other. Commitment was no longer confessions of everlasting love or assurances that their relationship was forever. It was being together and staying together through the hard times as well as the easy ones, and reaffirming to each other and to themselves that, through it all, their relationship always had come first and always would.

The course of the decision/commitment component of love in a close relationship depends in large part on the success of that relationship (and vice versa). Generally, the level of commitment starts at

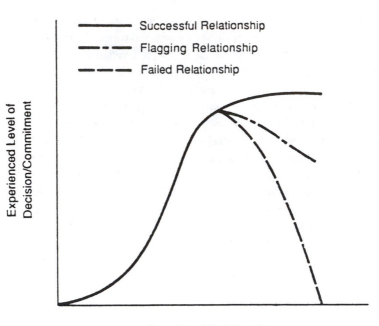

Figure 3.7. The course of decision/commitment as a function
of duration of relationship.

zero, before you meet the person, and then increases. Usually, if the relationship is to become a long-term one, the increase in commitment
in the decision/commitment component will be gradual at first and
then speed up. If the relationship continues over the long term, the
commitment will generally level off, yielding an S-shaped curve. If the
relationship begins to flag, the commitment will begin to decline; and
if the relationship fails, commitment may disappear entirely. Figure 3.7
shows the course of commitment graphically. As always, the smooth-
ness of the hypothetical curve does not take into account the tribulations of many relationships. As shown in Figure 3.7, even the most successful relationship has its ups and downs.

To conclude, the respective curves representing degrees of intimacy,
passion, and decision/commitment show somewhat different forms –
differences that can be even greater than shown here because of indi-

vidual differences in close relationships. Because of the different trajectories of the components of love over time, relationships will change over time.

"Happily ever after" need not be a fairy tale; but if it is to be a reality, it must be happiness based on different configurations of mutual feelings at different times in a relationship. Couples who expect the passion to last forever, or the intimacy to remain unchanged, are in for a big disappointment. Relationships are constructions that decay over time if they are not maintained and even improved. A relationship cannot take care of itself, any more than a building can. Rather, we must take responsibility for making our relationships the best they can be, and constantly work to understand, build, and rebuild them. One thing that can help us in improving our relationships is knowing where they stand. The Triangular Love Scale, described in Chapter 4, helps us do so.

4

Measuring the Triangle of Love

Love, as viewed by the triangular love theory, can be measured. To this end, I have developed a scale to measure each of the three components, which allows couples to gain a better sense of where each partner stands in a loving relationship. The scale can, in pointing out the specific differences between the loves of two members of a couple, be therapeutic by helping to pinpoint the areas where change is necessary and suggesting the kinds of action that might effect change. Thus, a couple may be brought closer together or at least to the point where each partner can understand and respect the other's differences.

In this chapter I reproduce a questionnaire I have used to measure love – the Sternberg Triangular Love Scale. In one of my studies, I sought to validate this new scale and simultaneously to validate the triangular theory.[1] Participants in the study were 101 adults from the New Haven area, comprising 50 men and 51 women, who answered an advertisement in a local newspaper. To be eligible for participation, the participants had to be over eighteen, describe themselves as primarily heterosexual, and either be married or currently involved in a close relationship with someone. They also could not have participated in one of our earlier experiments. The range in age of participants was from eighteen to seventy-one, with an average age of thirty-one. Lengths of close relationships ranged from 1 to 42 years, with an average of 6.3 years.

THE STERNBERG TRIANGULAR LOVE SCALE

Instructions

The blanks represent the person with whom you are in a relationship. Rate each statement twice on a 1-to-9 scale, where 1 = "not at all," 5 = "moderately," and 9 = "extremely." Use intermediate points on the scale to indicate intermediate levels of feelings.

The first rating should represent the extent to which the statement is *characteristic* of your relationship. In other words, to what extent would you say that this statement reflects how you feel in your relationship? The second rating should represent the extent to which the statement is *important* to your relationship. In other words, to what extent do you feel it is important that you should feel this way, regardless of how you actually feel?

Intimacy

1. I am actively supportive of _____'s well-being.
2. I have a warm relationship with _____.
3. I am able to count on _____ in times of need.
4. _____ is able to count on me in times of need.
5. I am willing to share myself and my possessions with _____.
6. I receive considerable emotional support from _____.
7. I give considerable emotional support to _____.
8. I communicate well with _____.
9. I value _____ greatly in my life.
10. I feel close to _____.
11. I have a comfortable relationship with _____.
12. I feel that I really understand _____.
13. I feel that _____ really understands me.
14. I feel that I really can trust _____.
15. I share deeply personal information about myself with _____.

Passion

16. Just seeing _____ excites me.
17. I find myself thinking about _____ frequently during the day.
18. My relationship with _____ is very romantic.
19. I find _____ to be very personally attractive.
20. I idealize _____.
21. I cannot imagine another person making me as happy as _____ does.
22. I would rather be with _____ than with anyone else.
23. There is nothing more important to me than my relationship with _____.
24. I especially like physical contact with _____.
25. There is something almost "magical" about my relationship with _____.
26. I adore _____.
27. I cannot imagine life without _____.
28. My relationship with _____ is passionate.
29. When I see romantic movies and read romantic books I think of _____.
30. I fantasize about _____.

Commitment

31. I know that I care about _____.
32. I am committed to maintaining my relationship with _____.
33. Because of my commitment to _____, I would not let other people come between us.
34. I have confidence in the stability of my relationship with _____.
35. I could not let anything get in the way of my commitment to _____.
36. I expect my love for _____ to last for the rest of my life.
37. I will always feel a strong responsibility for _____.
38. I view my commitment to _____ as a solid one.
39. I cannot imagine ending my relationship with _____.
40. I am certain of my love for _____.

41. I view my relationship with _____ as permanent.
42. I view my relationship with _____ as a good decision.
43. I feel a sense of responsibility toward _____.
44. I plan to continue in my relationship with _____.
45. Even when _____ is hard to deal with, I remain committed to our relationship.

EXPLANATION OF ITEMS ON TRIANGULAR LOVE SCALE

Items 1 to 15 are for measuring the intimacy component; 16 to 30, for measuring the passion component; and 31 to 45, for measuring the decision/commitment component. In order to obtain your score, add up your ratings for each of the component subscales and divide by 15. This will give you an average rating for each item. (In the scale as it is used outside the context of this book, the scale items appear in a random order, rather than clustered by component, as they are here.)

NORMATIVE INFORMATION FOR THE TRIANGULAR LOVE SCALE

Here is some normative information that we have collected. Separate information is presented for characteristicness and importance. Ideally, the extent to which a given statement is characteristic of a relationship should also be roughly the extent to which it is important to the relationship. The greater the discrepancy, the greater the potential for distress.[2]

Characteristicness

"How characteristic is the description in each statement of your relationship?"

	Intimacy	Passion	Commitment
High	8.6	8.2	8.7
Average	7.4	6.5	7.2
Low	6.2	4.9	5.7

Importance

"How important is the description in each statement to your relationship?"

	Intimacy	Passion	Commitment
High	9.0	8.0	8.8
Average	8.2	6.8	7.6
Low	7.4	5.4	6.5

The high scores represent approximately the top 15 percent of scores; and the low scores, the bottom 15 percent.

WHAT WE FOUND USING THE SCALE

In our study, differences between the sexes were not significant.

I used the statistical technique of factor analysis in order to determine whether the underlying structure of the questionnaire was what we expected. In other words, although the theory identifies intimacy, passion, and decision/commitment as major components of love, there is no guarantee that these three components are the only ones, or that the ratings people give when filling out the questionnaire will be in accord with the structure suggested by the theory. Factor analysis provides a way of determining whether the questionnaire does indeed measure these three components, or something else.

The factor analyses of both the characteristicness and importance ratings revealed three factors, which corresponded to commitment, passion, and intimacy (with the order indicating the strength of the factors). The large majority of items measured what they were supposed to. Although the items worked well generally, some (fifteen out of forty-five) did not perfectly fit into the pattern predicted by the triangular theory.

We also asked participants in our study to rate their satisfaction in their close relationship. We found that intimacy and passion scores predict satisfaction the best, followed by commitment. Intimacy, in particular, predicted satisfaction best in terms of happiness, closeness, rewardingness, and goodness of the relationship, and not because the satisfaction scale emphasized this component over any other.

In sum, these and other, more technical data provided quite good support for the triangular theory of love. The data might not have supported the theory, of course: The factor analysis might have supported some other theory (or no theory at all), and the components of the theory might have failed to predict satisfaction in relationships. But, in fact, the data were supportive. The theory is not only intuitively plausible but makes sense in terms of the empirical data. We can therefore use the theory and the scale with some confidence in understanding love in close relationships, recognizing that neither this nor any other theory will answer all possible questions about love. In order better to understand the meaning of love, we need to look at its history, which we do in Part II of the book.

Aiming Cupid's Arrow: Love over Many Lifetimes

5

The Prehistory of Love

The theory of evolution was first applied, of course, to biological organisms.[1] A fundamental question addressed by that theory is how human beings came to be. The evolutionary account is that, through a process of natural selection, organisms that were able to adapt to the environment survived and reproduced, and organisms that were not able to adapt met their demise before they were able to reproduce.

Over time, selective forces favored some genes over others. New kinds of organisms evolved through essentially random mutations, most of which hindered the ability of the mutants to adapt. But every once in a great while, a favorable mutation would occur, giving the mutant an advantage over existing species. Eventually humans evolved and were favorably endowed for adaptation to the environment.

Attempts were made in the nineteenth century to apply the theory of evolution to the social as well as the biological realm, but "social Darwinism" proved to be little more than an apology for the existing social order.[2] With little to contribute, the movement faded.

In the past two decades or so, new attempts have been made to adapt evolutionary theory to the social realm, in general, and to relationships, in particular. Several proponents of this viewpoint have proposed evolutionary accounts of love and attraction.[3]

According to this view, adult love is an outgrowth of at least three main tendencies.

The first tendency is the need of the infant to be protected by either its parents or substitutes for them. The parents need to show *commitment* to the infant, the important third component in the triangular theory of love. The evolutionary function of attachment is primarily protection from predators; people – whether children or adults – tend most to seek attachments when they are somehow threatened from the outside. For example, in wars, besieged nations seek allies; people who are threatened by legal action seek lawyers or other advocates; in families, when one member is somehow besieged, the family rallies often around the besieged member, even if, in the past, they have not been particularly close. Tragedy can bring together couples as well as families, although great stress can also tear a couple or a family apart.

One theorist suggests a close analogy between the attachment John Bowlby has studied in infants and the attachment that can be observed in adult lovers.[4] Bowlby observed the tendency of the infant to seek out – to attach to – the mother as a sort of security and as a haven from distress. According to this view, children imprinted on their parents, attaching to them in a way that they will not attach to any other adults; later, when these children become adults, they tend to seek lovers who resemble their parents in certain critical respects. People may be particularly susceptible to visual imprinting, so that they may even look for lovers who physically resemble the opposite-sex parent in significant ways. Basically, people's future levels and types of *intimacy* – the first component in the triangular theory – are partially determined in their infancy.

The second basic tendency – in some respects, the flip side of the coin – is the parental protection tendency. One seeks not only to be protected by one's lover but to protect him or her as well. Thus, men often are attracted to women who in certain ways resemble infants, such as in having big eyes and soft skin. These men describe their lovers as cute and cuddly, use diminutive nicknames, and often indulge in babytalk when being affectionate. Women, as well, often enjoy the "little boy" aspects of their boyfriends and husbands and use diminutive nicknames. The evolutionary function is the protection one gives to the other, and thereby to any children resulting from the relationship. Such protection depends on the *commitment* of one individual to another to be there no matter what.

The third kind of tendency is sexual and is thus most closely related to the *passion* component of the triangular theory. Sexual imprinting may develop around the age of three or four. Generally, although not always, imprinting is on a member of the opposite sex. But in the long term, imprinting for males and females does not necessarily result in comparable behavior toward the opposite sex.

Men may especially have an inclination toward short-term passionate sexual liaisons. In choosing sexual partners, they may tend to be less selective than women because they can rather easily spread their genes through sexual liaisons, and can continue to do so throughout much of their adult life. Their best bet is to choose women who will bear them children – women who are in good health, for which attractiveness and perhaps youth are proxies. Women tend to be more selective because they have limited opportunities to spread their genes. They ovulate once a month, and only prior to menopause, and can be impregnated only once every year or so; however, there is almost no limit to the number of women a man can impregnate, even within a short span of time. For women, given their limited opportunities, their best bet in terms of having the best possible children – genetically – is to be very careful about their choice of a man with whom to mate, and also about when they mate. They are thus likely to choose older men who have demonstrated their ability to acquire resources to bestow upon them and their progeny. They also are likely to choose men in whose commitment to themselves and their progeny they have confidence.

Our current civilization (at least in the West) encourages and generally legally only permits a unique marital commitment (at a given time) – monogamy. Two forces – a sense of morality and fairness, and stable living conditions for parents and children – propel us in this direction. For example, children have a more stable environment in a conventional home setting than when they are moved around with one parent from one lover to another.

The ultimate function of romantic love, from an evolutionary point of view, is to propagate the species, through sexual intercourse. Romantic love (intimacy plus passion) usually does not last long; and were it the only force keeping couples together, there would be trouble indeed in assuring that children are raised in a way that enables them to develop to their potential. Companionate love (intimacy plus commitment), or just plain liking, often helps a couple stay together and bring up the children after romantic love has died. But long-term liaisons may not be, evolutionarily, the natural state for humans. Indeed, some couples do decide to split up after their children are grown.

The greater unconditionality of our love for our children makes evolutionary sense in terms of the greater need of the child than of the adult for the parent to remain in the early years. Indeed, for some parents at least, some of the unconditionality of the commitment fades as the child gets older and no longer is as critically dependent on the parent.

Evolutionary theory is a bold attempt to place love within a broad biological framework. Obviously, it does not answer every question about love. At the same time, it provides answers that no other kind of theory of love has been able to address: for example, why love for young children seems to have a kind of unconditionality missing from other loves; and why we find babies cute, even when by some standards they might seem ugly. It is obviously of survival value to the species for people to find babies cute rather than ugly.

David Buss has suggested eight evolutionary-based goals of acts of love, all leading to increased reproductive success.[5]

1. *Resource display.* Reproductive success will increase to the extent that both the male and the female can find a mate with the most resources to commit. In many societies, a major resource of men is their financial success, which helps ensure the well-being of any offspring they father. A major resource of women is their attractiveness, which, research has shown, both generates passion and enhances the prestige of the man.

2. *Exclusivity: Fidelity and mate guarding.* In many species, the male and female guard each other from the sexual interest and passion of third parties – again, for an evolutionary reason. The female has a vested interest in the male's not having children with other females, lest her own offspring be deprived of some of the man's already committed resources. The male has a vested interest in guarding the female because her getting pregnant by another male will delay her pregnancy by himself. The male also might end up providing resources to someone else's progeny. Thus, fidelity fits into the evolutionary framework.

3. *Mutual support and protection.* Since offspring are dependent on their parents for intimacy nurturance, and many kinds of support, they benefit if the parents support and protect each other.

4. *Commitment and marriage.* To the question of why, with divorce rates so high, one should even bother with marriage, there is again an

evolutionary answer. Children from stable homes are most likely to thrive. Of course, a home with two parents can be more unstable and torn than one with a single parent, but marriage helps ensure that a breaking of commitment and subsequent parting of ways will not be whimsically undertaken. Indeed, almost all societies have customs and laws to make parting at least somewhat difficult.

5. *Sexual feelings.* Obviously, sexual intimacy and passion are necessary for reproduction to take place.

6. *Reproduction.* Since, from an evolutionary point of view, the goal of sexual intimacy and passion is the reproduction of the species, reproduction is a proximate goal of love acts.

7. *Resource sharing.* Resource sharing could be viewed as a form of mutual commitment, protection, and support, in that it enhances the environment in which children are raised.

8. *Parental investment.* Parental commitment to and investment in children is needed for the children to thrive and, ultimately, to be reproductively successful themselves.

The above goals make the point that, from an evolutionary point of view, men and women apparently want somewhat different things from a relationship. What, exactly, is it that each sex wants? A study by David Buss with fifty collaborators from around the world finds surprising similarities.[6] On average, women want in a man economic capacity, social status, age, ambition and industriousness, dependability, stability, intelligence, compatibility, size and strength, good health, love, and commitment. Men want youth, physical beauty, good body shape, chastity, and fidelity. It is important to add, however, that what men want in a casual relationship appears to be different from what they want in a long-term relationship, a fact that has been recognized throughout history and today as well.[7] In particular, chastity and fidelity are less of an issue in men's seeking of short- rather than long-term partners. Men thus seem more to emphasize passion-related elements, whereas women more emphasize commitment-related elements.

Not all scholars accept the evolutionary theory, of course. An alternative explanation of the data is that it is not female gender but low status that leads individuals to want the things that evolutionary theory suggests women want. According to this view, because women have lower status, they want those things that will bring them higher status.

Were men to have lower status, they would seek the same things in women that women typically seek in men.[8] The evidence on this hypothesis is mixed. On the one hand, there is some evidence that even in cultures where women have more status, they want the same things that women want when they have less status.[9] On the other hand, there is also evidence that higher-status women do have at least somewhat different preferences, caring less, for example, about money than do women of lower status.[10] Moreover, status has been shown to affect many kinds of interactions. For example, men interrupt women more than women interrupt men, on average. However, suppose we reverse the usual situation where the men are more powerful than the women. It turns out that, in this case, women interrupt men more than the men interrupt the women.[11] Clearly, power matters.

There are other aspects of interest in the data regarding the differences between men and women. For example, the differences in what men and women want appear to be larger for what people say they want through self-report than for what people exhibit in their behavior.[12] In other words, what people say and what they do may differ, and the differences may be larger for what they say.

Another ingenious study looked at men's and women's preferences in geographic areas that had either higher or lower rates of disease. According to one theory, it is not attractiveness, per se, that matters either to men or to women, but rather attractiveness as a proxy for freedom from disease. In areas with high levels of disease, physical attractiveness should be particularly important, because of the greater likelihood that individuals will be carriers of diseases that may interfere with their potential for reproductive success. In areas with low levels of disease, both men and women should value physical attractiveness less. That's exactly what the researchers found.[13] Of course, using physical attractiveness as a proxy for freedom from disease may have worked in the distant and even recent past, but it works only very poorly in the age of AIDS.

The jury is therefore still out on whether it is evolution or status within a culture, or something else again, that produces the patterns of data for men and women that we typically see. Let's turn now to the effects of culture, both on mate preferences and on what we mean by love in the first place. Chapter 6 considers these issues.

6

The History of Love
Revealed through Culture

Why have people been trying for countless generations to define what love is? Why, you can just look it up in a dictionary: "Love   n   1: strong affection   2: warm attachment   3: attraction based on sexual desire   4: a beloved person   5: a score of zero in tennis" (*Merriam Webster Dictionary* 1974).

Now you know why most people don't bother with a dictionary. Definitions of love always have seemed to be incomplete and dry versions of a sometimes explosive experience, which might cause anyone to wonder if the author of the dictionary definition has ever been in love. If so, he or she certainly hasn't applied the experience to the construction of his or her definition.

On the one hand, love always involves some combination of intimacy, passion, and commitment. On the other hand, how these components manifest themselves across different times and places may be different, even astonishingly so.

For example, in one time and place, an individual may view his or her partner's having sexual relations with a third person as tantamount to reneging on the marital commitment and as grounds for an immediate divorce; in another time and place, the very same action may carry no particular significance at all, and may be viewed as totally irrelevant to the marital commitment.

This chapter was written in collaboration with Anne E. Beall. The ideas are based on A. E. Beall & R. J. Sternberg, The social construction of love, *Journal of Social and Personal Relationships, 12* (1995), 417–438.

In one time and place, a man's telling a woman of his undying ardor for her and his desire to make love to her at the earliest available moment may be seen as the prelude to a serious committed relationship; in another time and place, the same actions may lead to a lawsuit or, at the very least, serious disciplinary action against the man.

Passion and commitment may be important elements of love, but their manifestations in the above situations show that what is considered acceptable as expressions of them can be tremendously variable across time and place.

How love is viewed always reflects a time period and place and, in particular, the functions romantic love serves and is supposed to serve there. More useful questions are, Why does love differ across time periods or cultures? or, perhaps, What is the function of love for a given culture?

Romantic love is important to a culture, although how it is important may differ somewhat from one culture to another. How love manifests itself is a social construction that is important to a society in numerous ways.

LOVE AS A SOCIALLY CONSTRUCTED IDEA

The Social Constructionist Approach

Love is a social construction. But what is a "social construction"? A social construction refers to the idea that there is no one particular "reality" that is simultaneously experienced by all people.[1] Different societies and different cultures have their own unique understandings of the world that are useful for people interacting within their society. Although they usually define love in terms of some combination of intimacy, passion, and commitment, or some subset of these elements, the combinations differ greatly across time and space.

Social constructionists differ from other theorists in their belief that people actively construct their perceptions of the world and use culture as a guide to do so. The social-constructionist perspective is that people are not passive recipients of a set of events in their environment. Rather, humans – and, in particular, human society – is actively engaged in determining what is "right" and "wrong," what is "moral" and "immoral." Thus, cultures are actively constructing social information all the time.

Culture is an important concept in the social-constructionist approach. Individual cultures provide people with a body of knowledge we call "common sense," which we use to explain events in the world. Thus, the ardent male mentioned earlier might be viewed in one place or time as a potential mate, in another, as a perpetrator of sexual harassment. What is viewed as a "commonsense" interpretation is different. Thus, cultures provide people with a set of lenses through which they can understand their environment. One's sense of the world is determined by these cultural lenses. The point of socialization is to teach children how to use the "lenses" the rest of the culture is using. These lenses are important because they provide people with similar understandings of the world and because they provide people with a way to interpret ambiguous information.

The social-constructionist approach has been applied to various aspects of human behavior, such as sexuality, relationships, and emotions.[2] For example, our modern conceptualization of grief is socially constructed differently across time periods.[3] The modern Western conceptualization of grief is that one has to "work through" the death of someone and that one then has to "let go" of a beloved. In the romantic age, however, many people held on emotionally to loved ones who had died, and their response to the death of the loved one was considered completely normal.

In the area of sexuality, too, cultures have different mores. Sexual practices are interpreted and reinterpreted across cultures, which explains why specific activities have acquired such divergent meanings over time.[4] Is anal intercourse disgusting, erotic, or a matter of indifference? There's no one answer: It all depends on time and place, as well as on the specific individuals who are making the judgment.

In regard to love, the social-constructionist perspective is that societies differ in their understanding of the nature of love. Cultures in different time periods have defined love quite differently. In some time periods, people have believed that love includes a sexual component, whereas in other eras people have believed that it is a lofty, asexual experience.[5] In the past two centuries, love has become a foundation for marriage, which is a relatively new development.[6] In the past, and even today in many cultures, marriages are arranged without any thought as to whether the two members of the to-be-committed couple will eventually experience intimacy or passion toward each other.

Typically, cultures recognize more than one kind of experience of love. Cultures may differ, however, in how they view these experiences and which experiences they consider ideal or even acceptable. For example, cultures may differ in their understanding of how and when passionate infatuation occurs or with whom one will become infatuated. Cultures may also disagree about how respectable certain kinds of feelings are for people to have toward each other.

In a very repressive culture, passionate sexual feelings may be acknowledged, but be viewed as a necessary evil. In a permissive culture, passionate sexual feelings may be valued and encouraged. There is no absolute right or wrong with respect to them.

Some Conceptions of Love

The history of the concept of love demonstrates how much a concept can change in even a short time. For example, in ancient Greece, many people believed that true love was the kind that occurred between a grown man and an adolescent boy.[7] Greek men were often contemptuous of their wives. Adolescent males, however, were considered highly attractive and worthy of the love of older men. Passion and even intimacy, two of the components of the triangular theory of love, were directed toward these adolescent males far more than toward wives (a fact not well explained by evolutionary theories).

An analysis of vase inscriptions from an ancient time period (530–450 B.C.) revealed that, of 925 erotic inscriptions, 91 percent of them were written by men to men.[8] Young men were so idealized that grown men would often use boys' gymnasiums as meeting places so they could watch seminude boys engage in physical sports.[9] Men also became romantically interested in women, but it was not their wives who excited their passion.[10] Men became interested in the highly stereotyped and even commercialized relationship they could have with a high-priced prostitute called a hetaera.[11]

Unfortunately, little is known about the love lives of women in ancient Greece, because there are few written records of women's lives and loves. The majority of women were not educated as much or as well as were men. Few women could read or write and the majority of women lived segregated from men.[12]

Some historians who have recently analyzed women's lives in ancient Greece suggest that women may have been the objects of love more often than was previously believed. For example, one researcher who has analyzed various Greek comedies contends that men's love for women may have been at least an ideal, although not one realized much in fact.[13]

In the nineteenth century, the ideal of many Victorians was of love between women and men, but a primarily asexual committed love. The Victorians were prone to believe that marital sex was a necessary evil, but one best consummated infrequently. Moreover, marital sex was believed to be permissible only for procreation.[14] Passion was to be directed toward God, not toward one's marital partner.

During this period, love and sexuality became dissociated. Good women were believed to have little interest in sexual activities. The last thing women needed was that lust take control of their marriages. Passion was fine, but sexual passion was a no-no.[15]

Love, in contrast to sex, was viewed as an experience that was ennobling, particularly for men, who needed ennobling influences. It was believed that women would civilize men and render them moral, despite their amoral nature.[16] Today there is a revisionist movement in interpreting Victorian sexuality, however, according to which at least some women are believed to have associated love with sensuality.[17]

In modern times, cultures have diverse and divergent conceptions of love.[18] In some modern cultures, love is viewed as an experience that can overcome any difficulties in a relationship, whereas in other cultures it is viewed as an experience that needs to be kept under careful control.[19] People surveyed in France reported that love is an irrational experience that takes control of a person and cannot be viewed objectively, whereas people in the United States reported that love is an experience that is important, but not necessarily uncontrollable or the only basis for a romantic relationship. In terms of the triangular theory, the French more emphasize the role in love of wild, unconstrained passion.

Modern conceptions of love can be so divergent that people in a given culture have difficulty understanding another culture's version of love. For example, many people in Chinese society view the current United States conception of love as quite aberrant.[20] In fact, the term *love* is generally used in China to describe an illicit liaison that is not socially respectable.[21]

These different views of love are probably due to the ways that the cultures view social relationships. American society is generally viewed as individualistic, whereas Chinese culture is collectivistic, with less emphasis placed on the fulfillment of one's own personal desires.[22] Rather, greater emphasis is placed on social relations with others. Many Chinese people appear to view themselves in terms of their social roles, such as mother, father, son, and daughter. They rarely view themselves as individual people looking for, or looking out for, their true selves.[23] Intimacy needs to be directed not solely toward a romantic partner but toward an extended family.

In Chinese culture, the individual emotional expressions that are valued in the United States may be viewed as unacceptable if they interfere with social relations. As a result, modern U.S. conceptions of romantic love have had little impact on Chinese culture.[24]

Reasons Love Varies across Cultures

One of the reasons love differs across cultures is because the experience of love is partially dependent on external factors, which are defined by the culture. As couples in relationships defined as illicit quickly find, it is difficult totally to screen out the effects of others. Indeed, such relationships may be kept going in part by the thrill of trying to screen out the effects of others who do not want to be screened out.

One external factor is simply the presence of a person regarded as socially desirable and as a suitable recipient of sexual feelings. When people are highly aroused and also in the presence of attractive confederates, they report experiencing romantic attraction and romantic love. The same arousal in the presence of someone not viewed as socially desirable leads to reports of various kinds of feelings, but not, typically, romantic ones.[25]

Of course, what is viewed as attractive and socially desirable differs across cultures. The features that may be considered attractive in one culture may be considered disgusting in another culture. For example, historically weight has been associated with desirability, but it clearly is not so viewed in the United States of today.[26]

In addition, factors such as social approval appear to influence the kinds of feelings and relationships people have with others. Cultures differ in the relationships to which they give social approval, which also can result in love being experienced differently across cultures. For example, in many periods of history, large age differences between men and women were considered routine. The older man could commit resources to the younger woman that a younger man could not commit. Today, large age discrepancies are often viewed as suspicious. Perhaps the older man is trying to prove to himself and others that he still has the virility to satisfy a much younger woman, or perhaps the much younger woman is trying to gain the fortune of the older man after he conveniently passes away.

Romantic involvement and love are strongly associated with support from one's social network of parents and extended family members. The more social support people experience for their romantic relationship, the greater people's satisfaction will tend to be with that relationship.[27] Familial support becomes increasingly important as a couple becomes more committed to the relationship.[28] This support may explain why people generally marry individuals of similar socioeconomic status and ethnicity.[29] In sum, some kinds of feelings and relationships are encouraged, and others discouraged, by one's social network. Although one can try to operate outside this social as well as cultural network, people have found through the ages that this is easier said than done.

It is difficult to operate outside the network in which one lives because love itself is a socially constructed idea. Although there is no one definition that adequately captures what is viewed as defining love throughout the ages or across cultures, four aspects seem important to it across time and space.

FOUR ASPECTS OF A CONCEPTION OF LOVE

Four aspects of love appear to be common in conceptions of love across cultures, although their contents may not be: (1) the beloved, (2) the feelings that are believed to accompany love, (3) the thoughts that are believed to accompany love, and (4) the actions, or relations between the lover and the beloved. Consider each of these aspects in turn.

The first aspect of love is the beloved. The objects of love change with time period and culture. For example, in some time periods, Christians believed that one should love God above anyone or anything else.[30] Of course, other loves were allowed, but many people believed (and some still believe) that the most suitable object of love was God.

In modern times, the most suitable beloved is generally believed to be an adult member of the opposite sex or, less frequently, of the same sex.[31] Today, many people believe that love of God and of another individual are complementary, although in some churches, such as the Roman Catholic Church, clergy are not allowed to marry on the view that they will then be in a better position to devote themselves more fully to God.

The second aspect of love is the feelings that are believed to accompany love. Modern views of love, in contrast with the Victorian ones described earlier, typically include a passionate sexual component and emphasize feelings of sexual arousal.[32] Of course, this view is not new. Sappho specifically described the physiological arousal that she believed accompanied love. Five centuries before Christ, she wrote about the feelings she had when she viewed the woman she loved:

> speak – my tongue is broken;
> a thin flame runs under
> my skin; seeing nothing,
> hearing only my own ears
> drumming, I drip with sweat.[33]

The third aspect of love pertains to the thoughts that are believed to accompany love. These thoughts are usually about the beloved. Throughout the ages, people have attempted to characterize these thoughts. Often these thoughts concern the welfare of one's partner or the desirable attributes that one's partner possesses.[34] Another common thought is the anticipation of being with one's partner.[35]

Philosophers dating back to Plato have described the thoughts they have believed people to experience during love. Plato suggested that people love a particular individual because that person represents an idea that one is seeking, such as truth or beauty.[36]

According to Plato, one would never love a person in that person's totality, because no person represents goodness or beauty in totality. At a certain level, one does not even love the person at all. Rather, one loves an abstraction or image of the person's best qualities. Plato never considered that one would love a person for his or her unique qualities, because the ideas are abstractions that do not vary. We thus look for the best embodiment of, say, universal truth, not for an idiosyncratic truth.

The Platonic view of love is not popular today. On the contrary, people today take a more Aristotelian view, wanting to love and be loved for who they are in the flesh. They want to direct their "triangle of love" toward a real person and not just toward an ideal. Indeed, people sometimes become alarmed when a lover seems to love them not for who they really are, but for some idealized abstract conception of who the lover would like them to be.

The fourth aspect of love addresses the actions, or relations between a lover and the beloved. Love has even been conceptualized in terms of a set of acts, such as supporting or protecting another person and showing one's commitment to him or her.[37] The action triangle, mentioned earlier in the book, points out that actions may or may not correspond to feelings. When they do not, the actions can be quite discrepant from the feelings generating them.

Other cultures have conceptualized love as a chivalrous, usually nonsexual relationship between a knight and a noble lady. Here, as in other conceptions, passion is largely separated from sexual experience. This kind of love is sometimes referred to as courtly love.[38] Generally, the knight would perform numerous feats to gain the attention of the lady. She might, if the knight was lucky, eventually acknowledge the knight as her knight. The courtly love relationship generally included no or, at most, little sexual activity.

In summary, love comprises four basic aspects: (1) the beloved, (2) the feelings of intimacy, passion, and commitment that are believed to accompany love, (3) the thoughts that are believed to accompany love, and (4) the actions, or relations between the lover and the beloved. But what each piece of information means can differ from one culture to another, as can its importance.

THE IMPORTANCE OF LOVE TO CULTURES

Love and Cultural Institutions

Conceptions of love are important to cultures because they implicitly define what is appropriate and desirable in human relations. For example, conceptions of love prescribe ways of thinking and acting toward one's beloved.

In general, when people are observing ambiguous stimuli, they are influenced by consensual ideas of what is true.[39] People will often say ridiculous things if they believe others accept these things, such as that a line that is obviously shorter than other lines is longer. Consensual judgments about the nature of love are even more powerful than those about fact, because there is no objective yardstick with which to conduct a precise measurement. What is normal is ambiguous and consensually defined, and there is no objective set of things one can do to show that the so-called "normal" isn't the way things should be. If only we had that yardstick! Should a man be allowed to fall in love with a married woman? It depends on the subjective yardstick society provides.

Not only society, but the person involved places constraints on who is considered an acceptable recipient of the person's love. Men and women may place different constraints on who is considered to be acceptable. Historically, sex differences have been found in the experience of love, which may be due to the different economic pressures men and women face. Some research has suggested that women are more pragmatic and less idealistic than men in their romantic relationships and in their experience of love,[40] although there are widespread individual differences and it is hazardous to generalize.

This sex difference may reflect, in part, differing reasons why men and women marry. Women, unlike men, historically are more likely to have married in order to have a certain life-style. Men may have had the luxury of marrying for love, whereas necessity may have led economic considerations to have predominated for women.[41]

Today, however, things are changing. Both men and women are more nearly equally emphasizing the romantic aspects of relationships.[42] Women have become more educated and have entered the paid labor force in large numbers.[43] As a result, they have generally become less dependent on economics for entering into a marriage and have increasingly concentrated on love as a reason for marrying.

In summary, conceptions of love serve many functions. Cultures help define the beloved, the thoughts, the feelings, and the kinds of actions that should accompany love. Love is more likely to be the foundation for marriage in individualistic cultures than in collectivist cultures. Love tends to be more important when kin networks and economic pressures do not determine whom one will marry.

Conceptions of Love and Their Relation to Time Periods

Because theories of love are also theories about people, love is strongly related to ideas about the nature of humanity as well as about the nature of the self. Today, love is often viewed, in part, as a means for self-discovery.[44] The discoveries may be of just how irrational one can be, at least when one is in love. But such a view, however acceptable it may be today, was not always viewed as acceptable.

During the Enlightenment, love was typically viewed as a rational and orderly experience that could be controlled by those who experienced it.[45] This notion is expressed in *The History of Tom Jones, A Foundling,* an Enlightenment novel. In the novel, a magistrate reproaches Jenny for losing her chastity. He informs her that she should not use love as an excuse for her behavior because "love, however barbarously we may corrupt and pervert its meaning . . . is a rational passion, and can never be violent."[46] Passion, and intimacy as well, were viewed as occurring in the cognitive domain rather than in the domains of feelings and motives.

Fielding was not the only one of this period who believed that love is a desire that can be fulfilled in a rational way. Philosophers such as Hobbes, Spinoza, and Locke believed that *love* is little more than a label that is applied to pleasurable experiences.[47] Spinoza once wrote: "Love is nothing else than pleasure accompanied by the idea of an external cause."[48] Locke also expressed the same idea when he said: "Thus any one reflecting upon the thought he has of the delight, which any present, or absent thing is apt to produce in him, has the idea we call love."[49]

The Enlightenment view of love as a rational experience reflected a dominant belief that humans are rational beings. People viewed humans as reasonable individuals who could be understood through science. The empiricism of Bacon and Locke led to a belief in natural law and a universal order in political and social issues.[50] People believed that through reason, the society would become more advanced.[51]

Love was assumed to have a rational basis because humans were viewed as rational. Thus, dominant ideas about the nature of humanity during the Enlightenment seemed to influence the Enlightenment conception of love.

In the eighteenth and nineteenth centuries, during the age of romanticism, people believed that love is uncontrollable and that men and women fall in love without reason. Kant argued that love cannot be controlled because it is a part of the senses.[52] Boswell likewise claimed that love is "not a subject of reasoning, but of feeling, and therefore there are no common principles upon which one can persuade another concerning it."[53] A rich description of love during this period was that of Henry Poor, who described love as "that sentiment which excites such a tumult in our hearts and such overpowering sensations through our whole frames."[54]

The idea that love is an uncontrollable passion reflected romantic ideas that humans are not totally rational, and that some parts of the human experience cannot be viewed in a logical way.[55] Hume, for example, believed that one could never determine causality rationally and that cause and effect were only inferred without good evidence from two events that occurred conjunctively.[56] Voltaire believed that the idea that everything is reasonable is ridiculous. In his book, *Candide*, Voltaire used satire to show that people are not very reasonable – that they are more a parody of reason – and that they are governed largely by prejudice and superstition.[57] Small wonder that the conception of love during the romantic period was of something that may have had much rhyme but little reason.

In summary, the conception of love seems to be related to the dominant view of human nature that takes hold in a given time period. For example, during the Enlightenment, the idea that love is a rational passion was related to the belief that humans are innately reasonable. During the age of romanticism, the idea that love is an uncontrollable passion reflected the belief that humans are not innately reasonable and are heavily influenced by their emotions.

UNDERSTANDING THE EXPERIENCE OF LOVE

Representations of Love

Conceptions of love provide an important means for people to understand their lives and their relationships. A representation of love provides people with a prototype with which they can compare their thoughts, feelings, and actions.[58] People may decide if they are in love by evaluating their possible beloved, their feelings, their thoughts, and their behaviors in an effort to see if they match cultural prescriptions of love. For example, if a person's feelings toward someone and the cultural prescriptions for love match, the person might decide that she is in love. Consider an example.

Nella Hubbard, a nineteen-year-old woman from the turn of the century, lamented: "Oh, why can't I feel as I want to, as I ought to?"[59] Hubbard's use of the word "ought" suggests her view that there was a desired way of feeling that she had not experienced, at least not yet. Other women also experienced the same feeling. Maud Rittenhouse refused a marriage proposal because "my ideal of love comes to me and tells me that I am not living up to it, that the love I have for you is not worthy of it – and that seems terrible to me. There should be no doubt."[60] Rittenhouse obviously believed that her thoughts and feelings did not conform to a cultural notion of love; as a result she could not accept her suitor's marriage proposal.

People may also evaluate a beloved to determine if they are in love. When the beloved does not match the current prescribed prototype of a beloved, people may reject the idea that they are in love. For example, in the late nineteenth and early twentieth centuries, women often had very intense same-sex friendships that included kissing and caressing.[61] The women frequently wrote about the intensity of their feelings in these relationships but did not appear to believe they were in love. Married women would write that they longed to hold, touch, and kiss one another. However, these women viewed their female friends as just friends and nothing more.

In these cases, the behavior, thoughts, and relationships were similar to the ideal of romantic love. However, these actions occurred between members of the same sex. Because the actions did not fit a prototype of love, they were not considered romantic. Had these women experienced identical feelings for or even identical behavior toward men, they may have come to a different conclusion.

Regulation of the Experience of Love

When the feelings one has do not match current ideas about love, one may regulate one's thoughts or feelings to try to bring them into congruence with the current conception of love. For example, one woman who lived during the twelfth century experienced sexual feelings and implored God to help her overcome these feelings. She wrote: "I burn, desiring what the heart desires. Cut through, O Lord, my heart's greed and show me your way out." Living in a time period when people believed that sexual feelings distracted a person from the highest form of love, the love of God, the woman tried to free herself of what she probably saw as unacceptable feelings.

Specific regulatory mechanisms can be applied to all emotions, including love. These mechanisms include (1) input regulation, which is the regulation of incoming stimuli, and (2) output generation, which is the regulation of one's response to situations that elicit emotions.[62]

Input regulation is a coping mechanism that is designed to regulate the stimuli a person experiences. When one regulates input, one selectively approaches or avoids objects that elicit an emotional response. In the case of love, people do selectively expose themselves to things that cause them to experience happiness and joy, and that seem to be promising leads to generate feelings of love.

When people regulate input, they often appraise a situation to make it appear more favorable than it really is. When in love, people frequently appraise their lovers and their relationships in ways that suit them. For example, a person may turn a blind eye to a lover's faults – which are often pointed out by friends and family – only to start noticing these faults when feelings of passion begin to fade.

People's choices of romantic partners are also regulated by their judgment of who is possible for them, and they may suppress emotions toward people who represent unrealistic targets. For example, at a given time, a divorced member of the royalty of one country or another may appear an attractive goal, but an unrealistic one that is not worth pursuing. Research suggests that people are generally attracted to individuals who are similar to themselves in attractiveness.[63] In one study, male subjects who were given false feedback that they had done poorly on an intelligence test acted more romantically toward an unattractive confederate. Male subjects who were told they had performed well on the test acted more romantically toward an attractive confederate.[64] Thus, subjects' attraction to a romantic partner was dictated by how they felt about themselves. Subjects evaluated their possibilities for romance and then adjusted their evaluation of the confederate.

Throughout history, people have distorted their appraisals of potential or actual romantic partners when it has been desirable for them to do so. In one study, men who were infatuated with an attractive confederate with dissimilar attitudes tended to distort the importance and dissimilarity of her attitudes. Infatuated men regarded her dissimilar attitudes more favorably than men who were not infatuated with her.[65]

Other evidence demonstrates how feelings of love in a committed relationship start to regulate emotions, including appraisals of attractive others. For example, once people are in a committed relationship, they often start to devalue attractive alternative partners. As people's commitment to the relationship increases, the number of potentially attractive partners they perceive decreases.[66]

People also selectively appraise their romantic relationships to conform to the romantic stereotypes of the society in which they live. Many people believe in passionate "love at first sight" and in "falling head over heels." They may want to fall passionately in love at first sight, and may try to convince themselves that they have, but the best available evidence suggests that the experience is not common.[67]

Environments may also encourage or discourage the experience and display of love. For example, people tend to marry others of similar socioeconomic and cultural backgrounds, probably in part because they are more likely to meet people from such backgrounds and in part because such partners are considered socially most acceptable.[68] When families provide support for romantic partners, love is experienced, on average, more intensely and for a longer period of time.[69]

Once they are in a relationship, couples help define and understand emotional experiences for one another.[70] For example, individuals may try to encourage their partners to experience their emotions as indicating sustained feelings of love. Members of a couple may also help one another devalue potential partners and label feelings of attraction toward others as temporary passionate infatuation or foolishness. This labeling may be accompanied by a warning that the feelings should not go beyond the temporary.

CONCLUSIONS

In sum, love is a social construction that reflects a time and place. Although feelings of intimacy, passion, and commitment are elements of love throughout the ages, how they combine and what combinations are labeled as love differ. There is no definition that describes love throughout the ages or across cultures.

Our perceptions of who is a suitable object of our love are also shaped by culturally defined conventions of acceptability. The same person who in one time or place might be viewed as suitable, in another time or place might not be. In the United States, for example, some states once had miscegenation laws that outlawed marriages across certain socially defined racial groups.

Our feelings of love concern (1) the beloved, (2) the feelings that accompany love, (3) the thoughts that accompany love, and (4) the actions, or the relations between the lover and the beloved. One cannot fully understand a conception of love in any time or place without knowing how people think about these four aspects of loving relationships. One can find out something about these conceptions and the corresponding aspects not only through a direct analysis of a culture, but through an analysis of the literature of a culture, which is considered in Chapter 7.

7
The History of Love Revealed through Literature

If it is to stories we turn to understand love, then we need to look not only at contemporary love stories, but at love stories throughout the ages – across time and across place. The importance of classical love stories is demonstrated by their endurance. People have been telling and retelling the classical love stories for centuries. These love stories not only provide interesting diversions, but they also shape our own stories about love, providing, as they do, prototypes for what love is supposed to be.

Although conceptions of love vary somewhat with space and time, certain universal themes seem to transcend both space and time. For example, the Greek myth of Pyramus and Thisbe provided a model for *Romeo and Juliet,* which in turn provided a model for the American musical, *West Side Story.* The story of Cinderella has both a Chinese counterpart, "The Golden Carp," and a Russian one, "Vassilissa the Fair." Themes that have been repeated so often deserve our special attention, because their popularity suggests that they have something universal to offer – a truth that transcends time and space. These fantasy stories provide building blocks from which we construct our own stories, whether they be fantasies or not.

People's ideal love stories derive, in part, from the canon of love stories they have heard, read, or seen enacted. The ideals we collect from old love stories can help direct us in our lives, but they can also lead us

This chapter was written in collaboration with Susan Hayden.

75

to disappointment. Many of the love stories we most cherish are unrealistic; indeed, it may be their lack of realism that we most cherish. When we try to put them into practice in our own lives, however, we may nevertheless be disappointed to discover just how unrealistic they are.

Juvenile literature is especially important in serving as a basis for adult assumptions about love. Children's stories often depict love in an idealistic and reassuring way, and the movies based on these books are often so reassuring as to be bland in comparison with the books that inspired them. For example, in the actual German story of Cinderella, pigeons peck out the evil stepsisters' eyes.[1] This particular scene, however, did not make it into the cartoon movie.

Today more children learn fairy tales from Walt Disney than from the Brothers Grimm, and movies and television are more important in conveying love stories to a popular audience than are books of tales. The blandness in the children's movies may deprive children of a broad understanding of love, just as the salaciousness of adult fare may deprive adults of a realistic conception of what love has to offer them. It's a difficult task to find anything in the media that has much to teach us about the realities of love.

If there is one thing anyone can learn from classical love stories, it is that we flatter ourselves when we think that we fall in love totally on our own. The love stories we have heard, and that have been carried on through the ages, set up expectations for ourselves and our partners at all stages of a relationship.

This chapter continues with the chronological theme of the book, which is indeed the way most love stories proceed! Let's consider first falling in love, then being in love, and finally, either staying in love or falling out of love.

FALLING IN LOVE

In most love stories, the hero and heroine fall passionately in love at first sight. Snow White's prince needs only one look at her to decide that he wants to be with her for the rest of his life (or at least to live with her happily ever after). He wakes her from an evil spell and says: "I love you more than everything on earth. Come with me to my father's palace. You shall be my wife."[2] This kind of instantaneous action is typical of love stories, because love is often seen as the result of sudden and even capricious divine intervention.

In mythology, Cupid (as he was called by the Romans, or Eros, as he was called by the Greeks) is depicted as a capricious, often blindfolded, young boy who shoots aphrodisiac arrows at both mortals and gods, resulting in the victims' falling passionately in love with the first person they then see (see the preface to this book). The idea of an archer is not limited to Greek and Roman mythology. The Indian god of desire, Kama, was also depicted as an archer.

The imagery of a person's being the target of an archer suggests several things – the swiftness of falling in love, the sometimes arbitrary choice of the beloved, the pain that love can cause, and some kind of external force that is calling the shots. Lovers fall in love with whomever the gods choose, rather than choosing for themselves. Throughout the ages, the idea of inevitability has been at the core of diverse notions of love and especially of love at first sight.

Shakespeare's *A Midsummer Night's Dream* plays on this theme. Puck dispenses a love potion, thereby assuming the role of Cupid. He plays a joke on his master's wife, leading her to fall in love with an ass. He also unknowingly makes a faithful lover fall in love with another woman. Helena, a woman who loves unrequitedly, explains her dire situation:

> Love looks not with the eyes, but with the mind,
> And therefore is winged Cupid painted blind.
> Nor hath Love's mind of any judgment taste;
> Wings, and no eyes, figure unheedy haste.[3]

Helena would love another if she could, but Cupid has imposed a blind, unrewarding love on her.

Divine causation introduces an element of inevitability into many classical love stories. A lover feels that the beloved is "The One" – the person with whom the lover is destined to be forever. Ideally, the beloved feels the same way. Usually, the beloved is hoped to feel this same way, right away.

This aspect of the ideal story is one of the most unrealistic commonalities in classical love stories and, when applied to modern relationships, one of the most damaging. If the beloved does not experience an exclusive, seemingly destined feeling of passionate love at first sight, the lover may be disappointed. It is as though the one chance for true love has come and gone. In reality, the beloved may only need more time to become acquainted and establish intimacy with the lover.

There is also a tradition of love stories in which falling in love happens only after a certain amount of time – after some degree of intimacy has developed. But these stories are less common. Interestingly, they often center around the action of telling a story. For example, it takes the Sultan of Arabia 1,001 nights to fall in love with his favorite storyteller, Scheherazade. Similarly, it is by reading together that Paolo and his brother's wife Francesca begin an affair in Dante's *Inferno*. Again, Tristan was Iseult's tutor before they fell in love; he taught her to read. In each of these stories, a teacher-student story becomes the love story.

Falling in love with someone at first sight has always been a risky venture, because it is so heavily dependent on the physical appearance of the beloved. A lover's vision may become supersensitive, as in *Love's Labour's Lost*:

> [Love] adds a precious seeing to the eye;
> A lover's eyes will gaze an eagle blind;
> A lover's ear will hear the lowest sound.[4]

Sometimes what the lover sees is not reality, however, but pure fantasy. The lover's vision may be distorted (even so far distorted so that the person becomes effectively blind, as Helena, quoted earlier, noted). The beloved may not be what he or she seems to be.

In the story of "The Disobedient Daughter," a West African (Ibibio) tale, Nkoyo, a willful and headstrong daughter, demands to marry a handsome stranger who is not at all what he seems. He is actually a skull who has borrowed his friends' body parts in order to appear handsome. Unknowingly, Nkoyo's parents agree to let her marry him. The stranger takes her to the Bush of the Dead, where he proceeds to dismember himself. When Nkoyo discovers that her husband is actually an ugly skull, she is horrified, but she is unable to go back home. She takes care of her mother-in-law, who teaches her that neither beauty nor love based on beauty can last.[5] The wise mother-in-law helps her escape and return to her family. Many Western stories of love do not convey this realistic warning against the perils of love at first sight, and leave off at "happily ever after." Love at first sight is often a poor basis for a lifelong commitment.

There can be a kind of cruelty in love at first sight. The common metaphor of archery implies the pain of the victim, the lover. The lover often does not will his or her falling in love, and may find the imposition of the gods to be painful or, at best, extremely inconvenient.

An illustration of this extreme inconvenience is in the story of Tristan and Iseult. Tristan falls in love with Iseult as he is about to deliver her to be the wife of his lord, King Mark.[6] It does not take much of a reality check to realize that both the choice of lover and the timing were poorly conceived.

Archers are often warriors and capture their victims. The theme of the beloved "capturing" the heart of the lover is a common one, and often, the lover then tries to capture the heart of the beloved in return. In the Cherokee story of "Why Mole Lives Underground," Mole decides to help an unrequited lover. He burrows under the beloved's house, takes out her heart, and instructs her unrequited lover to swallow it. The next morning, the beloved feels strangely attracted to the man and asks to be his wife.[7] The lover's capture can take other forms. In the Song of Songs, for example, a lover is held "captive" by his beloved's hair,[8] a theme that is also common in the artistic work of the great Norwegian painter, Edvard Munch.

Just as psychological research suggests that, initially, passion rules and people are first attracted by physical appearance, but then go on to look for other things,[9] so does classical literature show how a relationship that starts off being about physical appearance can become committed, enduring, and grounded in the spirit. The love of the Egyptian gods Isis and Osiris survives despite the fact that Osiris is castrated, chopped up into fourteen pieces, and thrown into the Nile. His physical state is irrelevant: His resourceful wife Isis still manages to conceive his child and be faithful to him,[10] a feat that is truly worthy of a god, but that might be quite a bit more difficult for anyone else.

Snow White is an extreme case in that only her beauty matters to her prince, but, as in many fairy tales, beauty and goodness are inextricably linked. To obtain beauty is to obtain goodness, a belief that persists in our society.[11] People have a passionate response, and assume that all the rest will go with it.

The protagonist of an Indian story, "The Perfect Bride," observes of his beloved: "When her figure is so beautiful, her character cannot be different."[12] Incidentally, the reason the bride is perfect is her hospitality. She is beautiful, but she is also a thrifty woman and a good cook: She manages to make the hero a whole meal out of a pound of rice, and then she lets him take a nap on her own bed. So he marries her. What else could a man want? This integration between food and love appears elsewhere in literature, most recently, in *Like Water for Chocolate*.[13]

Providing good food is just one way to deserve the affection of a lover. There can be many other signs of deservingness as well, some of them linked to the mouth but not to food. In the Native American (Teit) story of "The True Bride," a good and lovable bride spits gold, whereas an impostor spits foul-smelling toenails.[14] Which would you choose?

The tale of Cinderella, the Chinese story of "The Golden Carp," and the Russian story of "Vassilissa the Fair" are more orthodox examples of virtue rewarded. In all three stories, the virtuous daughter of a merchant is mistreated by her new stepmother and stepsisters. The virtuous daughter is forced to do the family chores, but neither her hard work nor the rags she wears spoil her beauty. In the story of Cinderella, a fairy godmother appears and gives Cinderella a dress so she can go to the ball. In "The Golden Carp," Ye Syan (Cinderella's counterpart) receives a dress from a magic set of fishbones.[15] Each of the virtuous women goes to a ball arrayed in her finery. A handsome prince dances with her, falls in love with her, loses sight of her at the end of the evening, and then finds her again using the shoe she left behind.

Vassilessa the Fair doesn't have things so easy: She must escape from the hut of Baba Yaga the cannibal. When she escapes and presents the tsar with twelve handmade shirts, he falls in love with her.[16] In all three of these stories, the audience realizes that the heroine is virtuous, but the royal hero falls in love with her for her beauty alone.

Virtue is not always assumed. In the stories of "The Frog Prince," "Beauty and the Beast," and the Zuni (Native American) tale of "The Serpent of the Sea," the heroes make the heroines prove their virtue. In all three stories the heroes are princes who, through enchantments, appear in animal form: a frog, a serpent, and a beast, respectively. They then make their demands.

The frog prince retrieves a golden ball for a princess and in return makes her promise to treat him as a playmate, even though he is ugly.[17] The serpent of the sea demands a greater price: The heroine must sacrifice herself to him for having violated his sacred spring.[18] When each heroine fulfills her task, the spell is broken, and the hero returns to (handsome) human form and marries the heroine.

The moral of the stories is that the woman is virtuous because the hero's physical appearance does not affect her behavior, and so she will love the hero for his character rather than for his appearance or his money. In every case, it is the man who tests the woman.

The sex roles are reversed in Shakespeare's *The Merchant of Venice, Twelfth Night,* and *As You Like It,* where Portia, Viola, and Rosalind, respectively, dress up as men to test the fidelity of their would-be mates. These stories indicate that beauty should not be the sole basis for a relationship – but beauty never hurts.

The classical love stories may emphasize beauty as a basis for attraction, but many of them go well beyond beauty to other qualities. The Indian story of "The Man Who Changed Sexes" shows that generosity and physical prowess can be just as attractive as physical beauty – that passion can be excited by attributes that go beyond looks. In the story, Princess Sasiprabha falls in love with Manahsvamin when he lifts her out of the way of a rampaging elephant.[19]

The *Kama Sutra* is replete with suggestions as to what is attractive and what makes a person desirable. According to its author, Vatsyayana, men who succeed with women are those who know the science of love: They know its sensual pleasures, they talk well and can tell stories well, they dress well, and they are strong. These characteristics, except for strength, are also admired in women.[20] The *Kama Sutra* includes tips on how to court a woman, and includes advice regarding the washing of the feet, buying off of the woman's servants, and pretending to be sick so as to encourage the woman to come and take care of you.

The *Kama Sutra* also includes a handy diagnostic list of the degrees of love a lover can experience, thereby enabling the lover to chart progress in the quest for the beloved. These degrees of love (or perhaps just its passionate component) are (1) love of the eye, (2) attachment of the mind, (3) constant reflection, (4) destruction of sleep, (5) emaciation of the body, (6) turning away from (other) objects of enjoyment, (7) removal of shame, (8) madness, (9) fainting, and (10) death.[21] Most people will probably be happy to achieve even the lowest degrees of love.

The inclusion of signs is in itself interesting, and a departure from the literary tradition. In that tradition, the hero and heroine generally know when they are in love. Indeed, they have no doubt. In real life, this kind of clarity is often absent. Setting oneself up with the ideal fairy-tale story may therefore lead, once again, to unrealistic expectations regarding what is likely to transpire in one's life.

Eventually, though, one recognizes that one has fallen in love. The next step is being in love, which we consider now.

BEING IN LOVE

Once the heroes of a love story have fallen in love, the narrator may pause to define love itself. In the Indian story of "Two Kingdoms Won," a courtesan explains love to a hermit she has seduced as "a certain incomparably pleasurable tactile experience of two persons, a man and a woman, who are both passionately interested in the object of this experience. The circumstances of Love are all things that are charming and beautiful."[22] Her definition includes the sensual pleasures of love, as befits her profession.

The *Kama Sutra* adds intellectual and spiritual dimensions, viewing love as "the enjoyment of appropriate objects by the five senses . . . assisted by the mind together with the soul."[23] But it retains a very strong sensual component of love, further defining love as "the consciousness of pleasure."

Although love is generally viewed as pleasurable, it can also produce frustration. Andrew Marvell's definition of love is decidedly gloomy: "It was begotten by Despair / Upon impossibility."[24] Such a depressing assessment of love would seem discouraging for most people. But Florentino Ariza, the hero of Gabriel Garcia Marquez's novel, *Love in the Time of Cholera,* has an answer after suffering fifty years of unrequited love: "Think of love as a state of grace: not the means to anything but the alpha and the omega, an end in itself."[25]

Ariza's view is of love as a circle. It is its own aim, and the process of loving is the goal. It falls back upon itself. In fact, the circle is the most common symbol of love next to the valentine heart (which, incidentally, is often shown as pierced by Cupid's arrow). The circle of a marriage ring also symbolizes and legitimizes the union between two lovers. Even two adulterous lovers, Tristan and Iseult, exchange a green ring as a symbol of their mutual fidelity. A circle also suggests regeneration and the cycles of fertility, linking love with sex.

Just as food can be used to entice the beloved, so can it be used to symbolize love already formed. The metaphor of food describes the sensual pleasure of being with the beloved, as well as the lover's fundamental need of the beloved (i.e., the lover needs love to live, just as much as he or she needs food).

In the Australian aboriginal story of "The Girl Who Made Dilly Bags," a quiet girl, Lowana, secretly loves a hunter named Yoadi. She gets left behind when her family travels to a far-off festival. Yoadi notices that she has been left behind and comes to get her. On his way home, he kills several animals to present to her. When she sees him, she almost faints out of both hunger and love. He gives her the food, watches her eat, and then announces that he will marry her. He then takes her to the festival to which her family has already gone.[26] The moral of this story is that if you love somebody, you feed the beloved; and if somebody feeds you, you may come to love the one who feeds you.

Other stories include more detailed descriptions of food intended to convey the sensual experience of loving. In the Song of Songs, a lover speaks to his beloved, saying: "Your brow is a fresh slice of pomegranate."[27] Similarly, the narrator of *Love in the Time of Cholera* uses food imagery to describe Fermina Daza seducing her husband: "She cut him to pieces with malicious tenderness; she added salt to taste, pepper, a clove of garlic, chopped onion, lemon juice, bay leaf, until he was seasoned and on the platter, and the oven was heated to the right temperature."[28]

Food's value as sustenance is emphasized in other stories. In the Persian story of Layla and Manjun, a chieftain's son goes mad with love for Layla, his schoolmate, earning himself the name of *manjun*, meaning "madman." He runs away from civilization, goes naked, and eats only grass. He explains his strange behavior, saying, "My body no longer has desire. Love is my fire and my essence. The bundle which is my self is gone. Love has entered my house."[29] Or, as the Beatles said, "All you need is love."

Manjun's description of love as fire is typical in love stories. In Indian mythology, the god of love, Kama, is often identified with the god of fire, Agni.[30] Fire is an appropriate metaphor for love because both spread quickly and are potentially destructive, as is proved in the West African story of "The Fire of Life." Alabe, a young girl, unwittingly walks into the sacred bush where the boys of her village live until they are initiated as men. She falls in love with a young man and seduces him. Unfortunately, he then dies for profaning the sacred bush. The chief proclaims that the youth can be brought back to life, but only if someone who loves him will rescue a lizard thrown in a bonfire. Both of the boy's parents try to rescue the lizard but shy away in fear. Finally Alabe runs into the bonfire and saves the lizard and the boy. Things do not work so well for Alabe, however: The tribe decides she must be punished for her original act and throws her into the fire.[31]

Society often seems hostile to love, especially if it does not conform quite exactly to the societal specifications. Nature, however, may support the loves that society rejects. In the Chinese story of "Cowherd and Weaving Maid," a cowherd marries a fairy, Weaving Maid, and they have two children. One day Weaving Maid's fairy grandmother decides to take her back to fairyland and throws down a silver river between the husband and wife. Cowherd is brokenhearted. A sympathetic flock of magpies saves the day, however. They intervene by interlocking their wings and forming a bridge so that the family can climb over and reunite. The fairy grandmother then decides to allow them to meet each year on the seventh day of the seventh month.[32]

The animal kingdom is similarly kind to Psyche in Greek and Roman mythology. Her mother-in-law, Venus (in Roman mythology, Aphrodite in Greek mythology), orders Psyche to perform three impossible tasks if she wants to see her husband, Cupid (Eros), ever again. She must rapidly separate a bushel of corn, millet, and wheat mixed together; obtain some golden fleece that is extremely difficult to obtain; and bring back water from the Styx, the river of death from which no one returns. In each case, Psyche is rescued by Nature: Ants separate the grain, marsh reeds whisper her instructions on how to obtain the fleece, and an eagle fetches her the water.[33] In this and other stories, Nature intervenes to protect true love.

Love is inextricably linked with nature because love and sex are related: Love is fertile. The fertility of love is especially emphasized in ancient myths because ancient civilizations were so dependent on Nature. In the Mesopotamian legend of Inanna and Dumuzi, love is linked to the flooding of the floodplain. As Inanna and Dumuzi make love, plants pour out of Inanna's womb.[34] More significantly, the cosmic and fertile love of the Indian gods Shiva and Sati ensures the rebirth of the entire universe.[35]

Although love is often depicted as a force of nature, it is expressed in many different ways socially, and the tradition of love stories includes a wide variety of ways in which people can love. There is no one story of love.

In the Indian tradition, love is often playful – a game story. The *Kama Sutra* even suggests that the lovers participate in games together.[36] Shiva, the Lord of Destruction, is described as playing with his wife Sati, braiding and unbraiding her hair, and picking her flowers.[37] In Greek stories, love is a game, but a more competitive one – it's more like a contest. Leander swims the Hellespont every night to be with his lover Hero until he drowns in a storm.[38]

A more modern parallel to the physical contests of the Greeks is the verbal sparring of Beatrice and Benedick in Shakespeare's *Much Ado about Nothing*. For this couple, "amor militiae species est": Love is a kind of warfare,[39] or war story. In fact, many of us have heard the expression, "You are so beautiful when you are angry."

The *Kama Sutra* includes entire chapters on techniques for striking and biting a lover, and gives advice on how to have love quarrels.[40] Perhaps the hope is that sanctioned outlets for conflict in a relationship may prevent real harm to either partner.

Often lovers do not compete against each other, but undergo together a test of their commitment, especially a test of separation. Romeo and Juliet are the most familiar example of lovers separated by their families.[41] Their mythological prototypes, Pyramus and Thisbe, were also separated, in their case, by a thick wall, the same idea used in the modern musical, *The Fantasticks*. Pyramus and Thisbe managed to communicate through a small crack in the wall, a scene that is parodied in *A Midsummer Night's Dream*.[42]

The plot of the Indian play *Shakuntala* revolves around a separation as well. King Dushyanta falls in love with a hermit's adopted daughter, Shakuntala. He consummates their love and then returns to the capital, where he forgets her because of a curse. When he comes to his senses and realizes that he has unknowingly rejected his true love, their separation becomes so painful for him that he almost goes berserk. A portrait of Shakuntala increases his passion for her. Finally the two are reunited at the end of the play.[43]

The portrait of Shakuntala illustrates the fragility of love: The beloved is irreplaceable but also unpossessable. Owning a portrait of her is futile because seeing her likeness only exacerbates the loss of her actual presence.

Pain is essential to love. We have seen that the metaphor of love as a result of a kind of divine archery conveys the pang of falling in love. There is the possibility of pain in love as well. A German proverb puts it well: "Keine Liebe ohne Furcht und Argwohn" – no love without fear and hate.[44]

We can see the connection between love and pain through etymology as well: The word *passion* comes from the Latin word meaning "to suffer," and the name of Tristan, the most popular hero in the troubadour tradition, means "sadness." Denis de Rougement goes so far as to write in *Love in the Western World* that "Happy love has no history. Romance only comes into existence where love is fatal, frowned upon, and doomed by life itself."[45] Here, de Rougemont's view is that passionate love requires a kind of emotional masochism, because the idea of passion is linked with suffering.

Love can be such a powerful force that suffering comes to seem worthwhile and even appealing. In the story of Layla and Manjun, Manjun's father takes Manjun to Mecca to cure him of his mad love. Instead of asking Allah to rid him of his love, Manjun wishes for even more love and more madness. He gets his wish, and having completed step 8 in Vatsyayana's sequence, he goes all the way to the top, and reaches step 10, dying on Layla's tomb.[46]

These extremes of love tend more to be associated in most people's minds with the young, although they are not limited to the young. Florentino Ariza's mother advises Florentino in *Love in the Time of Cholera* that he should suffer all he can while he is young, because this kind of suffering does not last one's whole life.[47] Florentino proves his mother wrong, however, by loving and suffering steadfastly for fifty years.

Various religious traditions also link suffering and love. In the Christian tradition, infinite hope opens the way for infinite suffering in love. For example, First Corinthians 13:7 reads "Love bears all things, believes all things, hopes all things, endures all things."[48] In Buddhism, Kama (desire) is the source of all suffering; the way to enlightenment is to banish desire.[49]

Love can cause great suffering, but the suffering is generally based in the individual's own construction of reality, which may have little to do with anyone else's construction. In most traditions, love is portrayed as a means of escaping reality. Sometimes it has a magical quality about it. To acquire love may require aphrodisiacs; to get rid of it may require exorcism. Its very lack of objective reality is what elicits so many sacrifices for love. One can never show that it truly does not exist.

True love, in the literary tradition, is rarely mundane. For example, it cannot be bought. In Shakespeare's *Antony and Cleopatra*, Cleopatra tests Antony by asking, "If it be love indeed, tell me how much." Antony replies, "There's beggary in the love that can be reckoned."[50] Love that can be bought, ironically, has no value.

The Greek myth of Endymion and Selene emphasizes love's dreamlike quality. Selene, the goddess of the moon, falls in love with an extremely handsome shepherd, Endymion. Selene asks the king of the gods to make Endymion sleep forever, so that he will dream of her in an eternal sleep of love.[51] Endymion's love is close to the perfect example of unreal, unreciprocated, and unconsummated love.

True love is typically viewed in the great love stories as spiritual, which puts it beyond the realm of the mundane as well as that which can be bought. The body is unimportant: True lovers may never even touch, as in the story of Layla and Manjun. In the Chinese story of "The Student Lovers," Yingtai disguises herself as a boy in order to be able to go to school. She meets a boy named Shanbo at school, and they become close friends and study partners. Yingtai falls in love with Shanbo but cannot reveal her disguise. Her parents summon her home and inform her that she is betrothed to someone else. Meanwhile, Shanbo learns that Yingtai is a girl and dies of grief when he realizes that he cannot marry her. She visits the grave on her wedding day, and it opens to receive her. According to the legend, you can still see two butterflies on the tomb, even today.[52] Through this metamorphosis, love overcomes death. In the Christian tradition, love conquers death: Christ's resurrection is God's ultimate demonstration of his love for the world.

The student lovers never even expressed their feelings for each other, let alone touched. Their love, like that of Pyramus and Thisbe, Romeo and Juliet, and Layla and Manjun, was consummated in death. This love is the purest form of spiritual love. Great love often has this ascetic quality. Manjun expresses it when he says: "My body no longer has desire. . . . The bundle which is my self is gone. . . . You do not see me. You see 'the beloved.' How then can love be torn from my heart?"[53] The spiritual union of lovers makes separation and even death bearable. Shakuntala's lover, King Dushyanta, says upon leaving her, "It is my body leaves, not I; / My body moves away but not my mind."[54]

The American poet Anne Bradstreet expresses the same mind–body duality in "A Letter to Her Husband, Absent upon Public Employment":

> If two be one, as surely thou and I,
> How stayest thou there, whilst I at Ipswich lie?
> . . .
> Flesh of my flesh, bone of my bone,
> I here, thou there, yet both but one.[55]

Their bodily separation is unimportant because their spirit is one. The spiritual fusion in love destroys the individual's selfhood in creating a new, shared self. Manjun demonstrates this fact visually by tearing in half a piece of paper with the names *Layla* and *Manjun* written on it. "With lovers, only one name is needed," he says.[56] The name stands for the combined self. To a lover, the union of love is more important than his or her own life. Love and self-sacrifice go hand in hand.

True love is above all altruistic. The Sumerian lover Dumuzi agrees to trade in half of his life to expiate his wife's crime against the gods of the Underworld.[57] In the Greek story of Alcestis and Admetus, Queen

Alcestis offers to die for love. King Admetus falls ill and an oracle pronounces that he will die unless someone agrees to die in his place. After searching in vain throughout the entire kingdom for a volunteer – even his parents turn down the offer – his wife Alcestis decides to die for him. She is ready to make the sacrifice, but the hero Hercules intervenes and wrestles Death for her life so the royal couple can stay together.[58]

The Native American "Legend of Multnomah Falls" describes a fulfilled sacrifice. A plague descends on a Multnomah village, and the shaman declares that only a pure maiden, the daughter of a chief, can save the people by throwing herself off a cliff and sacrificing herself to the Great Spirit. The only daughter of the head chief decides to do it when her own lover sickens; because of her death, everyone else recovers. A beautiful waterfall springs up on the cliff where she jumped.[59] Here, the waterfall is the physical realization of the fact that, in love, self-sacrifice is rewarded. Love provides its own justification for such self-sacrifice.

These sacrifices require an intense faith in and commitment to the beloved and an unswerving belief in love itself. It is not in human nature to suffer without cause. The Greek story of the musician Orpheus demonstrates the danger of losing faith in love. Orpheus's wife Eurydice is bitten by a serpent and dies on the first day of their honeymoon. Orpheus goes crazy with grief and decides to try to persuade the gods of the Underworld to bring her back to life. His music charms the Lord of the Dead, and the god agrees to allow Orpheus to escort Eurydice back to the world of the living, provided that Orpheus never once looks back to see whether she is following him. Orpheus leads Eurydice all the way to the top of the Underworld, but at the last second, he panics. He looks back, and consequently loses her forever.[60] Love requires a faith and self-restraint that Orpheus did not quite possess.

Often what gives lovers their faith in love is a feeling of destiny. Snow White can sing with certainty, "Someday my prince will come." Love in love stories is meant to be a once-in-a-lifetime event. Love is willed by the gods or by destiny, to the fortune or misfortune of the lovers, who have little or no say in the matter. The first words of *Love in the Time of Cholera* are: "It was inevitable."[61] Romeo and Juliet, too, were "star-crossed" lovers, destined for disaster.[62]

On a happier note, in Indian mythology, Shiva and Sati are made to be together forever. Their love transcends death as it endures through the cycle of rebirth: Sati is born again and again in different forms to be reunited with Shiva.[63] In the mind-set of love stories, there is one destined partner for every man and woman. Despite the fact that very few people will admit to believing in destiny of this kind, the mind-set underlying the belief is still very popular, and it may impose unnecessary and even unwise limitations on the idealist's love life.

As we have seen with Romeo and Juliet, love is in the stars – or isn't. Dante describes the cosmic force of love in the last line of the *Paradiso* of his *Divine Comedy:* "L'amor che move il sole e l'altre stelle" (Love that moves the sun and the other stars).[64] The Indian tradition describes love as the generative power of the universe. Kama is both the source from which we come and the object to which we go; desire is the source of creation.[65]

The spirituality, altruism, and power of love lend it the authority of religion. Florentino Ariza sees love as "a state of grace,"[66] and love is seen in many cultures as the ultimate human experience; it may therefore be associated with a higher being. Love is still sacred to many, even in our own more secular times. Gabriel Garcia Marquez remarks that "it is a pity to still find a suicide that is not for love."[67] Love is perhaps the only justification there is for suicide.

Love and religion can also complement each other successfully. Such complementarity is seen in Elizabeth Barrett Browning's poetry:

> I love thee with the passion put to use
> in my old grief's, and with my childhood's faith,
> I love thee with a love I seemed to lose
> With my lost saints – I love thee with the breath,
> Smiles, tears, of all my life! And if God choose,
> I shall but love thee better after death.[68]

Browning channels some of her formerly religious energy (her "childhood faith" and her "lost saints") into love, but she does not reject religion entirely. Rather, the mix of religious and romantic imagery is doubly charged.

In Sonia Sanchez's modern short story, "Just Don't Never Give Up on Love," an old woman on a park bench recounts her love life to the narrator. She describes the new lease on life that her second husband's love gave her with the imagery of baptism: "he just pick me up and fold me inside him. I wuz christen' with his love."[69]

The juxtaposition of religious and romantic imagery is not as dramatic in Hinduism, because Kama (desire, affection, love, lust, or sensual pleasure) is one of the four *purusarthas*, or goals of life.[70] (The other purusarthas are *dharma* – right conduct, duty, or virtue; *artha* – accumulation of wealth; and *moksha* – the release of the soul from the cycle of rebirth.)

In comparison with Hinduism, where sensual love is included within the bounds of religion, the Judeo-Christian separation of the two can seem artificial, although it makes for more drama when they are combined.

THE CONSEQUENCES OF LOVE FOR LOVERS

Love is a transformational force. In Ovid's *Metamorphoses,* the changes love brings about are physical. Pyramus and Thisbe become mulberry bushes with blood-stained berries. The god Apollo's unwilling love, Daphne, becomes a laurel tree. Adonis, Aphrodite's beloved, dies while hunting and is transformed into a flower, the anemone. These metamorphoses are not specific to the Greek tradition. The student lovers in the Chinese story by the same name turn into two butterflies on their shared tomb. In the Australian aboriginal myth of "The Rainbow and the Bread-Fruit Flower," two unhappy lovers turn into a rainbow and a bread-fruit flower so that they may be together without their jealous relatives.[71] In these metamorphosis myths, the lovers take on a new form in nature so that they may display their love forever.

Love may transform the personality rather than the physical state of a lover. In the love-story tradition, love often tends to make men adventurous and women patient. Men go out and slay dragons for love; women keep the hearth fires burning. Penelope, in Homer's *Odyssey,* is the paragon of the faithful wife, waiting almost twenty years for her husband, Odysseus, to return home.[72]

Lovers of both sexes acquire courage from their passion. Leander is unafraid to brave the waters of the Hellespont to see his beloved Hero;

Alcestis is unafraid to die for Admetus.[73] In the Bible, John 4:7 reads, "There is no fear in love; but perfect love casteth out fear: because fear hath torment."[74]

Ironically, a lover may display symptoms of fear such as muteness and paralysis in the presence of the beloved on account of the intensity of his or her feelings. These symptoms do not indicate a real lack of courage in the lover; the devaluation of the body in great love makes physical harm seem irrelevant.

The courage instilled by love renders a lover capable of overcoming any obstacle. The Japanese story of "Elimination" illustrates the extremes to which a lover will go, both to create obstacles and to overcome them. The hero Heichu is so desperately in love with the lady-in-waiting Jiju, who has spurned him, that he decides to try to diminish his love for her by seeing the contents of her chamber pot. When he finally acquires the chamber pot, however, he drinks what is inside and falls even more in love with her.[75] His attempt to use an elimination to eliminate his love thus fails. More commonly, lovers are tested by separation or societal disapproval than by their reaction to the chamber pot.

In the myth of Pyramus and Thisbe, continued in *Romeo and Juliet* and in *West Side Story,* the lovers are forbidden by their parents and by society in general even to see each other. Their love survives in spite of or perhaps because of these obstacles. Edith Hamilton notes in the case of Pyramus and Thisbe that love "cannot be forbidden. The more that flame is covered up, the hotter it burns."[76]

In the "Knight's Tale" of the *Canterbury Tales,* Chaucer proclaims that love provides its own laws.[77] And in love stories, the law of marriage often seems to get the least respect, because marriage often has so little to do with love and often opposes it. Tristan, Manjun, and Lancelot all loved married women. Love can be politically as well as morally subversive because it is democratic: Everyone is capable of love. Love does not observe social boundaries of class, race, or religion. Love's all-justifying omnipotence makes it easier for lovers to disobey the laws of society.

The rebellion of a lover against society is sometimes diagnosed as madness, or at least irrationality, as in the case of Marius in *Les miserables.* In fact, whether a lover intends to rebel against society or not, his or her actions may seem crazy because the normal mind-set is upset by love's passion. Shakespeare's Rosalind declares, "Love is merely a madness, and, I tell you, deserves as well a dark house and whip as madmen do: and the reason why they are not so punished and cured is, that the lunacy is so ordinary that the whippers are in love too."[78]

Many people experience what feels like temporary insanity when they are in love, but few experience it to the degree that Manjun, the Persian hero, does. He goes to the desert, eats only grass, wears no clothing, and speaks to animals. During the time he is in the desert, however, he composes his best poetry. Shakespeare also notes the connection between artistic creativity and madness in *A Midsummer Night's Dream*: "The lover, the lunatic, and the poet / Are of imagination all compact."[79] Love may drive a lover crazy and inspire that lover at the same time.

Often great lovers write great literature or music. Their favorite subject, of course, is love, or their beloved. Dante and Petrarch are perhaps two of the most famous examples of literary lovers, but we really have no way of knowing how many poets have written out of love. Denis de Rougemont explains the poetic urge in love: Passion "tends to self-description, either in order to justify or intensify its being, or simply in order to keep *going*."[80] Dante managed to keep his love for Beatrice going for his entire lifetime.

Artistic expression of love is not always merely descriptive. In the Native American Brule Sioux "Legend of the Flute," the narrator explains that playing the flute, the *siyotanka*, is the way for young warriors to court their *winchinchala*, their sweethearts.[81] However, the inspirational force of love has its limitations. Ironically, even the most eloquent poet may become mute in the presence of his or her beloved.

Something about love transcends words, a perhaps ironic statement in a book about love. Narrators of love stories often find themselves leaving much to the imagination of the reader or listener or even apologizing for what they cannot put into words. Gottfried von Strassburg, the adapter of the German version of Tristan and Iseult, is candid about his own deficiency in describing the relation between the lovers. When Tristan and Iseult elope and hide out in the Cave of Morois, Gottfried explains that he cannot tell what happened in the cave, because only the lovers themselves know.[82] When lovers get down to the business of

loving each other on a spiritual plane, the narrator often resorts to us-
ing figures of speech to describe their state. The configuration of words
in figures of speech suggests more than the words themselves denote.
For example, chiasmus suggests enclosure or combination of opposites.
There is a double chiasmus in Gottfried's version of the Tristan and
Iseult story:

> Ein Mann, eine Frau, eine Frau, ein Mann,
> Tristan, Isolde, Isolde, Tristan.
>
> (A man, a woman, a woman, a man,
> Tristan, Iseult, Iseult, Tristan.)[83]

This chiasmus is a verbal embrace. The figure of synesthesia expresses
the intensity of the love.

In the *Song of Songs,* a lover declares to his beloved that "The sound
of your name is perfume."[84] Similarly Shakespeare's sonnet number 23
pronounces that "To hear with eyes belongs to love's fine wit."[85] Love
also lends itself to oxymorons, given that it produces both happy sadness and pleasurable pain. Both synesthesia and oxymoron demonstrate the confusion and difficulty of a lover's attempting to express his
passion in ordinary language. Manjun expresses the wordlessness of
love using a metaphor: "The name is only the veil. Layla is the face under the veil."[86] Despite the wordlessness of love, lovers and storytellers
keep talking about it. By talking about love, lovers encourage themselves and others to pursue it. They spread the word in an evangelistic
fashion. Perhaps they are also trying to impose words and time on love,
but love opposes them both. True love is timeless, as Shakespeare's Sonnet number 116 suggests:

> Love's not Time's Fool, though rosy lips and cheeks
> Within his bending sickle's compass come;
> Love alters not with his brief hours and weeks
> But bears it out even to the edge of doom.[87]

One of the easiest ways to distinguish true love from its imitations
is to recognize the patience of true love: Lovers who are obsessed with
time are not concerned with spiritual pleasures. The *carpe diem* school
of poetry emphasizes the rush of time and the approach of death:

Gather ye rosebuds while ye may
Old time is still a-flying;
And this same flower that smiles today
Tomorrow will be dying.[88]

Now let us sport us while we may,
And now, like amorous birds of prey,
Rather at once our time devour
Than languish in his slow-chapped power.[89]

Herrick and Marvell are afraid of death and time because both destroy
carnal love. Carnal love is ephemeral, but true love "bears it out even
to the edge of doom."

FALLING OUT OF LOVE

Although love stories have far more to say about falling in love than
about falling out of it, we can nevertheless learn something about concepts of how people fall out of love. We can also learn about inau-
thentic kinds of love – the kind of love in which we should not engage.
For example, *Madame Bovary* describes love that is socially motivated
as false. But when she attempts to construct her own love life in the romantic tradition, she finds that no one lives up to her expectations, and
she commits suicide out of disappointment.[90]

La Rochefocauld states acerbically that "Il y a des gens qui n'auraient
jamais été amoureux, s'ils n'avaient jamais entendu parler de l'amour":
Some people would never have been in love unless they had heard others speak of it.[91] Ideally, love is a natural rather than a social phenomenon. Obviously, we cannot escape social influences, but we should not
get caught up in preconceived, inflexible notions of love. Love is often
associated with some of the cardinal virtues of society: truth, beauty,
and virtue, for example. But love can tolerate and overcome untruth,
ugliness, and even evil. Love is not a hard and fast quality; it is too large
and too complex to pin down. Many lovers have tried to impose their
love on the objects of their desires, but real love is not forced. Much to
the despair of an unrequited lover, love comes only of its own free will.

Unrequited loves are all the more tragic because we expect the
beloved to love the lover, according to the love-story tradition. In fairy

tales, it is assumed that a woman will love the prince who declares his love for her. Snow White barely has time to open her eyes before she promises to marry a man she has never seen before, only because he tells her he loves her.[92]

In the Native American story of "The Princess Who Rejected Her Cousin," the coy princess tells her suitor-cousin to cut open his right cheek if he loves her. The next day she tells him to cut his left cheek, then cut off all of his hair. When he presents himself, she laughs and refuses to marry such an ugly person. She is punished for her behavior, because he eventually regains his beauty and she loses hers.[93] She wrongs him by tormenting him, but her crime was not loving him in the first place.

The assumption that love will be reciprocated is often proved false in real life, sometimes with disastrous consequences: obsession or stalking, for instance. Spurned or abused love can easily turn sour. The cousin in the story of the princess who rejected her cousin does not take revenge on the princess; instead, the gods punish her. In Greek tragedy, the wronged partner takes matters into her own hands: Clytemnestra kills her adulterous and murderous husband,[94] and Medea kills her own and her deceptive husband's children.[95] In a perverse way, these actions are part of the love these women bore their husbands. Their love has turned to hate, but they are still acting out of the same intense passions that generated their love in the first place.

The end of love in love stories often leads to the suicide of either partner. The failure of love destroys a world – the emotional world that two lovers built around their intimate union. Life without a loved one means alienation in the literal sense of the word: The lover is turned into an "other," instead of being a part of a "we." Sometimes lovers feel that if they cannot be united with their loved ones, then they do not want to live alone in a divided state. Even the Bible maintains that life without love is futile, although it certainly does not advocate suicide. First Corinthians 13:1–3 reads:

If I speak in the tongues of men and of angels, but have not love, I am a noisy gong or a clanging trumpet. And if I have prophetic powers and understand all mysteries and all knowledge, but have not love, I am nothing. If I give away all I have, and if I deliver my body to be burned, but have not love, I gain nothing.[96]

STAYING IN LOVE

Some loves do succeed, and some couples stay committed and in love for their entire lifetimes. However, most love stories do not describe the evolution of love in time. Fairy tales do not deal with the "happily ever after" of old age or even middle age. They do not give advice about how to make love last, or how to maintain love from day to day. The chase is more dramatic than marriage or maintenance, and the details of domestic life are generally considered unworthy of literature, especially in the Western tradition. So how is it that successful lovers maintain their love in the absence of a tradition of maintenance of love? Telling stories of love inspires and rekindles love. In order to keep love going, we reinvent it for ourselves.

Because love depends on storytelling for inspiration, we need to be selective about what kind of stories we invent, repeat, or imitate. We should strike a balance between rejecting ideals that are impossible to achieve and maintaining our high standards. After all, we should not underestimate the power of love.

"Love is as strong as death. / Its passions are as cruel as the grave / and its flashes of fire are the very flame of God," says the Song of Songs.[97] Perhaps we need more stories about how to maintain love. There seems to be a taboo of some kind on love stories about old people in our culture, but the divorce rate in the United States and elsewhere certainly suggests that there is a need for models of lasting love – for stories that do not end with the "happily ever after" prescription that has no content.

There are some hints in the literature. The African American story of "The Lion and the Ashiko Drum, a Fable from South Carolina" gives a few suggestions about making love last. A guardian spirit gives Loaat the drummer advice about how to content his restless and homesick wife Tsara: "You want the Tsara of yesterday, but yesterday is gone. Look at your wife as she is today. Have patience, and you will see the crops will grow, the laughter will flow, the harvest will come, and there will be little dancers for your drum rhythms."[98] The hero's overall well-being depends on his love for his wife. If love goes well, then everything else goes well. This story reminds us that the ultimate reward for maintaining love is happiness. Love requires faith, suffering, and sacrifice, but its joys defy both time and death.

Perhaps the difficulty of expressing the spiritual state of being in love makes it impossible to describe how to stay in love. However, this difficulty has not stopped centuries of poets and storytellers from trying to express their love. In studying their works, we can garner bits and pieces of information that we can use in our own lives. All cultures acknowledge that love is desirable. Therefore, it is surprising that love stories generally do not attempt to address the question of how to maintain something so precious. Instead, they focus on falling in love, being in love, and falling out of love. The wordlessness of spiritual love makes explanation seem impossible, and the magical quality of love makes domestic details seem irrelevant. Perhaps in order to stay in love we need to follow the pattern dictated by the stories themselves and fall in love over and over again (with the same person). Then again, perhaps we need to know something that is not contained in the stories and that we must learn for ourselves. In the meantime, we can keep listening and reading for clues, because storytellers certainly believe that they have something to teach us, and most certainly they do.

We often think of others as the storytellers who tell us stories throughout our lives. But we, too, are storytellers, writing our own stories of love in our lifetime.[99] In Part III, we consider love in our own lifetime, starting in Chapter 8 with the role of childhood and adolescence in the development of love.

Firing Cupid's Arrow: Love in Our Lifetime: Beginnings

8

The Role of Childhood and Adolescence

Childhood affects our later choices of love in many ways. One of these ways is through attachment.

ATTACHMENT THEORY

Evolutionary theorists, as noted earlier, link romantic love to attachment and develop this link within an evolutionary framework.[1] Phillip Shaver and Cindy Hazan have greatly expanded upon this view of love as deriving from infantile attachment, and have proposed a theory of romantic love as attachment. They borrow the attachment concept from John Bowlby, but extend it by showing that styles of romantic love correspond to styles of attachment among infants for their mothers, as explained by the theory of attachment styles proposed by Mary Ainsworth and her colleagues.[2]

Ainsworth observed that infants, when separated from their mothers and placed in a strange situation with someone unknown to them, tended to react in one of three ways. Secure infants could tolerate brief separations and then would be happy when the mother came back; they seemed to have confidence that their mother *would* come back. Avoidant infants seemed to be relatively detached upon their mother's return; they seemed more distant from their mothers and less trusting of them. Anxious-ambivalent or resistant infants had great difficulty tolerating the separation and would cling to the mother upon her return, at the same time that they would show ambivalence toward her.

Attachment styles are not only powerful within a lifetime, but across generations. Research has revealed that attachment styles tend to cross over three generations – from grandmothers to infants,[3] and that they tend to be stable throughout the life-span.[4]

According to attachment theorists of love, romantic lovers tend to have one of the three different styles in a relationship.[5] A person's style is a matter of individual differences, and derives in part from the kind of attachment one has had to one's mother when young.

Secure lovers find it relatively easy to get close to and achieve intimacy with others. These people can be comfortable in depending on others and in having others depend on them. They do not worry about being abandoned or about someone getting too close to them. Intimacy is easy for these lovers.

Avoidant lovers are uncomfortable being close to or intimate with others. They find it difficult to trust others completely and to allow themselves to depend on others. They get uncomfortable when anyone gets too close, and often find that their partners in love want to become more intimate than they find comfortable. Intimacy is difficult for these lovers. It now appears that there are actually two kinds of avoidant lovers.[6] One kind is "fearful," and is afraid of getting close to and feeling intimacy toward others. The other kind is "dismissive," and simply prefers to keep an arm's length from others. These lovers reject intimacy.

Anxious-ambivalent (resistant) lovers find that others are reluctant to get as close as they would like. They often worry that their partners do not really love them or want to stay with them. They want to merge completely with another person – a desire that sometimes scares others away. The level of intimacy they have never seems to be enough.

It is hazardous to evaluate attachment styles as good, bad, or anything else. Indeed, attachments researchers have been criticized as using labels that seem to value certain attachment styles (e.g., secure) and devalue other styles (e.g., avoidant). Indeed, although the prevalent style of attachment in the United States is the secure style, in other societies, it is not. For example, the avoidant style is more common in Germany, the anxious-ambivalent style, in children of the Israeli kibbutz and from Japan.[7] Nevertheless, one empirical result may have some relevance to this debate: People with a secure attachment style are quicker to recognize words representing positive interpersonal themes, whereas people with other attachment styles recognize negative words more quickly.[8] The participants in this study were North American: Other results might have emanated from participants growing up and living in other societies.

Research shows that about 53 percent of adults are secure, 26 percent avoidant, and 20 percent anxious ambivalent, proportions that correspond roughly to those of the three kinds of attachment relation in infants.[9] But there are other aspects of the self that develop during childhood that can affect our later preferences in love.

SELF-ORGANIZATION

Research by my colleagues and I has suggested that, from a relatively early age, people start to develop ways of organizing how they think, learn, and more generally, process information. In particular, people develop diverse styles of thinking and learning.[10] They develop these styles by watching role models, by viewing the media, and no doubt, by bringing their personalities into interaction with the world. It's important to keep in mind that styles are not abilities. People at any level of ability can have any style. Rather, they are ways of using abilities – preferences for how to bring abilities to bear on our lives.

I refer to my theory as a theory of mental self-government, because the theory refers to how people govern and organize themselves, much as a political theory might deal with how societies organize themselves. Most relevant to us, however, is that certain styles of self-organization tend to be more or less compatible with other styles in other people. Consider some of the dimensions along which people differ, based on this theory.

Functions

One aspect of the theory deals with three different functions of mental self-government.

1. A *legislative* person likes to create, formulate, and plan for the solution of problems. This kind of person likes to do things his or her
   own way, and not be told what to do or how to do it. The legislative person is basically the type of person who likes to create.
2. An *executive* person is an implementer rather than a creator. This
   kind of person likes to follow rules or, at most, figure out which of
   several different given ways of doing things should be applied in a
   given situation. The executive prefers to work with a given structure, rather than to create the structure.
3. A *judicial* person is a judge. This person likes to evaluate people and
   what they do. The judge would rather evaluate a set of rules than
   either dream them up or follow them. This individual is likely to
   evaluate structures and then only follow them if they suit his or her
   tastes.

People are not "purely" one style or another, but rather, have preferences that tend to emerge in many, but certainly not all situations.
How do these three styles, which start to form during childhood, trans-
late into later success in relationships? I believe that one of the most
common and generally successful pairings is of the legislative with the
executive. The legislator is primarily responsible for deciding what to
do and sometimes, for deciding how to do it. The executive may decide how to do it, but usually is responsible for getting it – whatever it
may be – done. The pairing tends to be successful because each individual capitalizes on the tendency that the other individual lacks. The
legislator makes sure that there is a plan; the executive makes sure the
plan is implemented.

To the extent that there is a risk in this pairing, it is that the legislator will get bored with the executive, or that the executive will become
resentful of the legislator. In the former case, the legislator tires of
someone who seems to be a follower rather than a leader like himself
or herself. The legislator craves the companionship and intimacy of
someone more like himself or herself. In the latter case, the executive
becomes resentful of always seeming to be the one to follow orders. He
or she may not want to give them, but may not want to feel bossed
around either, which can start to happen in this pairing.

The legislator–legislator pairing has the advantage of being exciting.

Both individuals are creators, and so the sparks really can fly. There is more excitement and more variety as new ideas may be generated on an almost continual basis. The downside of this kind of pairing, however, is its greater potential for friction than is found in the legislator–executive pairing. In the legislator–legislator pairing, both individuals may want to have the ideas, but neither may want to implement them. The upshot may be that there is no agreement as to what should be done, and no one to do it, in any case.

Another common pairing – perhaps the most common – is the executive–executive pairing. The pairing is so common because our society, like most others, generally most rewards children for showing the executive style. The "bright" kid, the "good" kid, and the "easy" kid have in common that they do what they are told, and do it well.

In the case of the executive–executive pairing, both individuals prefer to be given direction. Such couples are likely to take the lead from the outside. They are likely to follow whatever the trends may be in housing, dress, food, exercise, or whatever. When we think of couples who try to keep up with or beat out the Joneses, their next door neighbors, chances are we are thinking of an executive–executive couple.

We know that other people's perceptions of approval or disapproval of a relationship strongly affect whether the relationship is likely to survive or not.[11] The executive–executive couple is probably the most sensitive to other people's approval or disapproval, because it is their style to value so much what others think and say.

Yet another pairing is the judicial–judicial pairing. Such couples can do extremely well together so long as they devote their judicial resources to evaluating other people and couples. They can go to a dinner party, for example, and spend many happy hours afterward evaluating all of the people at the party, as well as what they did and said at the party. Partners in this couple can run into trouble, however, if they turn their judicial tendencies inward toward themselves. When they start evaluating each other, they risk tearing their relationship apart.

Yet another pairing is the legislative–judicial. This pairing has one enormous advantage over others. There is someone to come up with the ideas for where the relationship should be going and what the couple should be doing; and there is someone to evaluate whether the ideas are any good. Many times, legislative people are quicker to come up with ideas than they are to evaluate those ideas. This pairing thus helps guarantee that good ideas will be accepted and bad ideas rejected.

At the same time, this pairing has an obvious inherent flaw. The legislative person is likely to feel criticized much of the time. The legislator's impression is likely to be correct, too. Two things can cushion the relationship. First, if the judicial individual is skilled in relationships, he or she may find a way to deliver his or her evaluations in a way that is nonthreatening. But if the person is not so skilled, there is a substantial potential for conflict. Second, if the legislative person is not defensive and is accepting of critique, then he or she may not even feel threatened by the judge. One or the other of these cushions would seem to be important for this kind of pairing, however.

The final pairing we will consider here is the executive–judicial pairing. This pairing may have the least potential for success. The executive person is likely to take the lead from the outside. The judicial person is likely to criticize that lead. But the judicial person may not have any viable alternative ideas of his or her own. The result may be a relationship in which there is a kind of stalemate. The ideas that are out there don't work, but there are no new ideas coming from within the relationship either.

Styles of thinking and learning, like styles of attachment, are important because they form in childhood and then continue throughout the life-span. Let's consider next how love plays itself out over this life-span, turning in Chapter 9 to a consideration of the role of adulthood in the development, maintenance, and dissolution of love.

9

The Role of Adulthood

With whom do we fall in love once we enter adulthood? A number of variables have been found to affect whom we end up loving. We'll consider some of those variables first, and then some of the theories about the effects of these variables.

VARIABLES AFFECTING ATTRACTION

Physical Attractiveness

Do we feel attracted to and often passionate about the most attractive person we can find, or do we feel attracted to someone whose attractiveness is roughly comparable with our own? Most people would probably assume we pursue the most attractive person we can find. Indeed, there is evidence of a "beauty-is-good" effect, whereby we ascribe goodness to those who are attractive.[1] The effect appears to be only moderate, however and, moreover, it is not equal across all kinds of goodness. It is largest on the dimension of social competence (i.e., our thinking that attractive people are socially competent), intermediate on the dimensions of intellectual and personal competence, and weak to nonexistent on the dimensions of integrity and concern for others.[2]

Society also apparently bestows an advantage on physically attractive people. Research shows that people who are physically unattractive earn less than people who are average in looks, who in turn earn less than people who are physically attractive.[3]

Of course, there are differences in people's conceptions of who is attractive. The correlation between people's judgments of who is attractive is only modest, and people's perception of their own physical attractiveness is also only modestly correlated with other people's perceptions of their physical attractiveness.[4] At the same time, the correlations are not zero. One group of researchers found that when native Asian and Hispanic students who had recently arrived in the United States, as well as white students who had been in the United States a while, were asked to judge the attractiveness of Hispanic, black, and white American women, there was a high degree of consensus in who was rated as attractive by all three groups making judgments.[5] In general, judgments of facial attractiveness are quite similar across cultures.[6] Curiously, research shows that the face judged to be the most attractive is the most "average" one. When photographs of people's faces are averaged by computer, the greater the number of faces averaged, the more attractive the resulting computer-generated face is judged to be.[7] Overall, consensus attractiveness is certainly, on average, an advantage to people in reaching many, although not all, goals they set for themselves.

According to the *matching hypothesis,* people look for partners not who are the most attractive possible but, rather, whose level of interpersonal attractiveness, broadly defined, matches their own. A test of the matching hypothesis involved a "computer dance," in which a large number (376, to be exact) of college men were paired with an equal number of college women.[8] They were each informed that the basis of the pairing was their profile of scores on a personality test administered at an earlier session when they signed up for the dance. The setting, therefore, was seen by these men and women as similar to that provided by standard computer-dating services.

In fact, the individuals were randomly assigned to each other, the sole restriction being that men were paired with women. The researchers collected information about each person so as to try to determine what aspects of the pairs would lead to greater or lesser success on the initial date at the computer dance. The idea was that people who were better matches would enjoy their date more; and the question addressed was,

What constitutes a better match? Unbeknownst to the individuals, each had been rated on physical attractiveness at the initial session in which the personality test had been given. After the date, each person was asked to complete a brief questionnaire assessing the date.

Only one factor influenced how much a person liked his or her date, how much a person wanted to see the date again, and how often the men actually asked the women for future dates. That single factor was the physical attractiveness of the date: The more physically attractive the date, the higher the ratings. Not even matching effects were found, whereby people liked dates whose attractiveness matched their own. Rather, almost everyone preferred the more physically attractive dates.

Why was physical attractiveness so important? After all, few people would admit to counting physical attractiveness so much in their choice of people to date or in how much they enjoy dates. Consider two reasons. First, unlike most personal attributes, which take some time to judge, physical attractiveness is registered immediately; thus it is one of the few attributes that can be assessed with any accuracy after a first date. Second, because contact on a first date tends to be superficial, the superficial aspects of a person are likely to be salient. If you really want to get to know someone, therefore, don't count too much on the first date. Or if you do want to go beyond physical attraction, don't count on mixers. You probably will find out very little and are likely to rely pretty heavily on physical attractiveness, not the establishment of true intimacy.

One possibility, of course, is that the sole importance of physical attractiveness and the failure of the matching hypothesis were due to the fact that partners were assigned. In the normal course of life, people choose their dates and risk rejection when they ask someone out. The risk of rejection may cause people to play it safe and to look for partners who match themselves, rather than those who are highly attractive physically. Because the dates in this study were assigned, neither partner had to risk rejection by the other.

In another experiment, individuals again were led to believe that they were signing up for a computer date.[9] Half the people signed up under conditions similar to those of the previous study, in which they were led to believe that they would go to the dance with their assigned partners. The other half were led to believe that their prospective dates would have the chance to turn them down after a short meeting. Although there were no differences in effects of physical attractiveness between the two groups, the researchers did find that more physically attractive individuals wanted more physically attractive dates – a result consistent with the matching hypothesis.

The investigators then asked individuals to choose a date from six photographs of members of the opposite sex who varied in physical attractiveness (according to independent raters). The possibility of rejection again did not affect the preferred level of attractiveness of the date; but, consistent with the matching hypothesis, more attractive individuals chose more attractive photos for their dates.

Other work also provides support for the matching hypothesis.[10] In one study, judges rated the physical attractiveness of photos of ninety-nine couples who were either engaged or going steady, as well as the attractiveness of a set of couples consisting of randomly matched men and women. Couples who were actually involved with each other were rated, on average, to be more similar in physical attractiveness than couples who were not involved with each other.

Two apparently opposing stereotypes seem to exist side by side in our culture. One is that what is beautiful is good, and vice versa. Perhaps its most famous expression is Keats's "beauty is truth, truth beauty." The opposing view is that you should not judge a book by its cover, or that beauty is only skin deep. According to this view, superficial beauty often is a cover for shallowness and lack of emotional depth, whereas superficial plainness may hide a gem in the rough. Indeed, people who are not physically attractive may well need to develop their internal resources so as to compensate in some way for their lack of physical attractiveness. Which view is correct?

One study required college men and women to rate photographs of three people of varying physical attractiveness on a large number of characteristics.[11] Half of the individuals rated same-sex photos; the other half, opposite-sex photos. The more physically attractive people in the photos were judged to have better personalities, greater marital happiness, more occupational success, more social and professional happiness, and more happiness in life than the less attractive people. There was no evidence of jealousy, although the investigators tested for it by trying to see whether raters might belittle very attractive photos

of members of the same sex as making the raters look bad by comparison.

Looks definitely matter not only to men, but to how men are perceived. When a male is associated with an attractive female, he makes
a much more favorable overall impression on people and is better liked
than when he is associated with an unattractive female.[12] This better
impression is made on both males and females. A beautiful woman thus
may have a radiating effect on the man associated with her. People often say that some men choose beautiful women in order to enhance
their own attractiveness – as, for example, the marriage of Aristotle
Onassis to Jacqueline Kennedy.

If people associate good looks with so many good things, do good
looks affect the way a person's work is judged, independently of the
work? In one study, individuals rated the quality of an essay when a
photo of the writer was attached to it.[13] The photos attached to the essays varied in attractiveness, but the same essay was used in each case.
A given subject saw each essay paired with only one photo. Dis-
turbingly, more attractive-looking persons received better ratings on
their essays, independent of the actual quality of the essay. In short,
physical attractiveness can bias the way in which a person's work is
judged.

It is sometimes said that Richard M. Nixon lost his televised debates
with John F. Kennedy as much for physical appearance as for anything
else. Kennedy looked relaxed and "up"; Nixon, tense and "down." Part
of the latter's problem was that his heavy beard left him with a pro-
nounced "five o'clock shadow." Bob Dole, too, struck a rather poor
figure – physically – in comparison with Bill Clinton. Who could doubt
that more physically attractive candidates have an edge?

The effects of physical attractiveness may differ for men and women.
Female spouses tend to be evaluated for physical attractiveness independently of their husband's physical attractiveness, whereas evaluations of the husband are affected by the wife's attractiveness. When an
unattractive man was married to a beautiful woman, it was assumed
by the subjects that he must have some exceptional compensating qualities – for example, high income or high occupational status.[14]

In evaluating potential mates, men place more value on women's
physical attractiveness than women do on men's.[15] However, not all

men appear to count physical attractiveness equally. In one study, investigators contrasted the importance of women's physical attractiveness to men who were either high or low in an attribute called *self-monitoring*. High self-monitors are people who tend to tailor their behavior to the situation, in the sense that they act one way with one person and a different way with another person so as to maximize their fit with each. Low self-monitors are more consistent in behavioral interaction: They tend to act more or less the same way no matter whom they are with. Their attitude is, "This is who I am, and you can take it or leave it."

Men who were high self-monitors valued looks more than did men who were low self-monitors.[16] Moreover, when men were given a choice between dating a woman described as physically attractive but not terribly nice versus one who was physically not very attractive but really quite nice, high self-monitors preferred the more physically attractive date whereas low self-monitors preferred the less physically attractive date who was described as being the nicer person. Thus, high self-monitoring men may be more concerned with the radiating effect of a beautiful woman than are the low self-monitors.

Once you think you know about a person's physical attractiveness, your judgments about them may be affected by that knowledge, and these judgments may actually create a self-fulfilling prophecy, affecting the way the person acts toward you. Investigators monitored a ten-minute phone conversation between a man and a woman. The men and women were previously unacquainted and were given the opportunity, allegedly, to get to know each other.[17] The men were each shown a photo of the woman to whom they were talking. Half the time the photo was of a beautiful woman and half the time, of a very unattractive woman. Unbeknownst to the men, the photos were not of the woman to whom each was talking. The conversations between the men and the women were recorded, and judges who never saw the photographs that each of the men saw rated either the men's or women's conversation on several dimensions.

The judges listening to the males' part of the conversation judged the men who thought they were talking to the attractive women as more social, sexually warm, permissive, interesting, and attractive than the men who thought they were talking to the unattractive females. Similarly, the judges listening only to the females' part of the conversation judged the women who were thought to be attractive by their male partners as more sociable, poised, sexually warm, and outgoing. In other words, when the men thought that they were talking to a very attractive woman, both they and the woman seemed more attractive in the phone conversation than when the men thought that they were talking to an unattractive woman. Thus, women who were thought to be beautiful and were treated as though they were beautiful reacted in a more attractive way and made the men act more attractively. Belief can become reality. People especially try to transform their beliefs into reality when they are aroused.

Arousal

Some men who pursue women have adopted a version of a very old trick: To arouse a woman's interest in them, they take the woman to some event that is emotionally stimulating, such as a wrestling or boxing match. For many women, of course, a good ballet or play may have a better effect. The goal is for the emotional arousal of the event to act as an aphrodisiac to stimulate passion. Does the trick work?

A study testing this idea was conducted in an unusual setting – a scenic spot frequented by tourists, which had two bridges in different places.[18] One bridge extended over a deep gorge and swayed from side to side while people walked across it. For most people, walking across this bridge was terrifying. The other bridge was stable and not high off the ground. Walking across it did not arouse anxiety. Male participants were assigned to walk across one bridge or the other, and as they walked across the bridge, they were met by an assistant of the experimenter, who was either male or female. The assistant asked each person to answer a few questions and to write a brief story in response to a picture. The picture was from the Thematic Apperception Test, a test for measuring personality needs. After the individuals wrote the story, the research assistant gave them his or her phone number and remarked that they should feel free to call the assistant at home if they would like further information about the experiment. The stories were then rated for sexual imagery. The highest level of sexual imagery in the stories was obtained by those men who walked across the anxiety-evoking suspension bridge and were met by a female assistant. Moreover, men in this condition were more likely to call the research assistant at home.

This research supports the stereotype that people who endure stress together are likely to be attracted to each other. Indeed, many passionate "office affairs" start with two people being brought together by their sharing of a common stress and their resolving their problems together.

A second study showed the effect of arousal in an anxiety-provoking setting.[19] Male participants came to participate in an experiment. Some of the participants were told that they were about to receive a series of strong and painful electric shocks; others, that they would receive only weak and nonpainful electric shocks. While they were waiting, the male participants were introduced to a young woman who was alleged to be another participant in the experiment, but who was in fact "planted" by the experimenters. While the participants were waiting to receive the shocks, they were asked to fill out a questionnaire evaluating the young woman. Participants expecting to receive the strong and painful shocks evaluated the woman more favorably than did participants who expected to receive the weak and painless shocks. None of the participants ever really received the shocks, which were mentioned merely as a device either to arouse or not to arouse the participants. Arousal, though, clearly serves to generate physical attraction.

Arousal can happen very fast. Evidence suggests that people start feeling expectations about romantic possibilities toward others within a fraction of a second of meeting these others.[20] In other words, passionate love at first sight is really at first sight, possibly starting to arise in a mere matter of moments.

Arousal is usually associated with feelings of romance. There is evidence that men and women may view romance differently. In particular, men seem, on average, to be more romantic than women, and to be quicker to fall in love than are women. Women, in contrast, tend to fall out of love faster than do men.[21]

The difference in experiences of romantic arousal is found not only between men and women. Research has shown that people who are high in self-esteem but low in defensiveness experience romantic love more frequently than do people who have other combinations of self-esteem and defensiveness. At the same time, however, people who are low in self-esteem tend to have more intense romantic feelings and also to find them to be less rational than do people with higher self-esteem.[22]

Proximity

Of the potentially millions of partners with whom one might become involved in a romantic relationship, one meets only a tiny fraction. Many of us choose a future mate on the basis of having met and truly gotten to know less than a dozen contenders, and it is the rare person who meets, and gets to know well, more than two dozen. The most important factor determining whom you meet and thus with whom you can become intimate is also the simplest – proximity. You are most likely to meet those people to whom, for one reason or another, you are physically near. In the age of the Internet, "virtual" proximity is becoming an important factor in whom we can meet.

A study investigated patterns of friendship among military veterans and their wives who lived in two student housing projects at the Massachusetts Institute of Technology.[23] The two housing projects had different architectural designs, so that it was possible to investigate the effects of proximity in two fairly different settings. People who lived closer to each other were more likely to establish intimacy and become friends than were people who lived farther apart. People who lived in centrally located apartments were more likely to form more friendships than were people who lived in apartments toward the end of a floor. Predictably, the friends of the people living near the middle of the hallway tended to be people on that floor. People living in apartments near stairways were much more likely to make friends with people living on the floor above, because they were in a position to interact with these people when they were going up the staircase. In choosing a place to live, you are also choosing a set of people with whom to live.

A second study used a dormitory situation for students at the University of Michigan.[24] For each of two years, seventeen male college students lived in a dormitory without rent in exchange for participating in a study on the formation of friendships. During the first year of the study, physical proximity did not influence interpersonal attraction. But during the second year – with an entirely different set of people living in the dormitory – proximity did affect attraction, with roommates liking each other more than did those who did not room together.

What might have caused the discrepancy between the results during the two years? During the first year, roommates had been assigned at random; during the second year, room assignments were based on a matching of the individuals' values and attitudes as expressed prior to their moving into the dormitory. Half of the students were assigned to live with others whose initial attitudes agreed with theirs; the other half were assigned to live with those whose initial attitudes were quite different. Regardless of assignments, though, the general effect still held: Roommates were more likely to be friends than were nonroommates.

In another study, researchers mailed questionnaires to fifty-two students in the Maryland State Police Training Academy.[25] The students were asked to name their three closest friends in the force after their six-week training. In the academy, students were not randomly assigned to seating and placement in classes. However, the basis of assignment was alphabetical order of last names, which hardly seems like a basis for forming friendships. Nevertheless, alphabetical ordering had a strong effect on friendship. Of sixty-five friendships, almost half were formed between trainees whose last names began with the same or adjacent letters.

Part of liking another person may be merely exposure to that person and nothing more.[26] Indeed, one study showed that even liking for unpleasant-tasting substances increases upon repeated exposure to them.[27]

On the other hand, there is the view that familiarity breeds contempt – that getting to know a person too well can lead to the downfall of a friendship. It can, as shown by a study conducted in a middleclass condominium complex in California.[28] Proximity was associated both with greater liking and with greater disliking. Moreover, the effect of proximity was greater on disliking than on liking: whereas 62 percent of people's friendships were with other residents in the same area, 70 percent of people's dislikings were also in the same area.

One of the more interesting studies of the effect of familiarity was done more than fifty years ago.[29] People were asked to give their impressions of groups of various nationalities, including the Danerians. Of course, the Danerians differed from the other groups in a critical respect: They were fictitious. There is not and never was any group called the Danerians. This fact did not stop participants in the study from describing the unfamiliar Danerians as possessing a number of undesirable qualities!

Whether familiarity breeds positive or negative feelings may depend on several things, such as whether the person is rewarding and punishing, whether one experiences arousal in the company of the person, and even whether you expect the time you spend with the person to be enjoyable or not. Thus, it may not be familiarity per se that matters, but what happens during the time you familiarize yourself with a person. These happenings may lead to intimacy, or they may lead to contempt.

Reciprocity

We tend to like those who like us, or, to be exact, those we believe to like us. Expressions of intimacy thus lead, on average, to further expressions of intimacy.

In one study, people who were previously unacquainted with each other were formed into small discussion groups.[30] Prior to their formation, each person was informed individually that, on the basis of personality-test information (which was phony), the experimenters were able to tell that certain members of the group, but not others, would be very attracted to that person. An informal group session was then actually held at a first meeting. After this meeting, the experimenter told the members of the group that they might eventually be paired off, and so asked them to rank each of the three other members of his or her group in terms of preference as a potential discussion partner. The whole group continued to meet for a total of six sessions, and a similar ranking procedure for preferred-discussion partners was obtained after the third and the sixth as well as after the first session. The investigators found that, at the end of the first session, participants preferred as potential discussion partners those other group members whom the participants had been told would like them on the basis of the phony personality-test data. Thus, the belief that another will like you can lead to your liking that other. By the third session, however, the effect of the phony data had disappeared, as participants were now in a position to discover whom they genuinely liked and who liked them. In a related experiment, when participants were evaluated by another person, their evaluation of that other was strongly influenced by the way in which they had been evaluated by him or her.[31]

Reciprocity appears to be important in the area of self-disclosure. Generally, people are more likely to like and feel intimacy toward others who are willing to show themselves as they really are.[32] When we bare ourselves to another, we usually expect that person to do the same. If someone does not, we feel uncomfortable and less attracted to him or her.

The findings on reciprocity show that one tends to get back what one gives. People who exploit others are usually recognized as exploitative, sooner or later, and then others react to them in kind or just start to shun them. In the long run, exploitation is probably not in your own self-interest in a relationship, even if you take a selfish point of view, because when you are eventually found out, you will likely get back what you gave. Of course, the Golden Rule may work on the average, but it does not necessarily work in individual cases. Some people take and give nothing in return. Others are able to give but reluctant to take.

Similarity

Do "birds of a feather flock together"? Yes.

Similarity can take many forms, several of which increase interpersonal attraction, in general, and intimacy, in particular. Demographic variables matter: Similarity in age, religion, education, physical health, ethnic background, economic background, and self-esteem increase interpersonal attraction.[33] People who are attracted to and who feel intimate toward each other also tend to have similar personalities, and having similar personalities is associated with marital satisfaction.[34] Attracted couples are also more likely to be similar in attitudes than are unattracted ones.[35] As noted earlier, couples in ongoing relationships are also more likely to be similar in physical attractiveness than are couples matched in age but not in physical attractiveness.

In one set of studies, participants, generally college students, start off by answering questionnaire items intended to measure their personality attributes and attitudes.[36] The participants are then shown the questionnaire of another individual whom they have not met. Unbeknownst to them, the unknown participant is a phony, and his or her responses have been manipulated so as to be either similar or dissimilar to those of the genuine participant. The genuine participant is left to form a general impression of the other person and to rate him or her on an Interpersonal Judgment Scale. The scale contains several items, two of which are critical: One regards personal feelings toward the unknown other, and the other regards the participant's willingness to work with the other in an experiment. Ratings on these two items, added together, are considered to be a measure of attraction toward the phony other. Scores on the Interpersonal Judgment Scale are predicted by the amount of similarity between the participant's and the phony other's patterns of responses. In particular, similarity in attitude is an excellent predictor of attraction as measured by the scale.

Why does similarity matter for attraction? Consider four reasons.[37] First, people may find similarity to be rewarding to them, in and of itself. Second, similarity may increase self-esteem: Hearing someone express similar attitudes or values may enhance your view of yourself, as through similarity you may receive support for the positions you take in life. Third, similarity may portend a bright future: People may have greater confidence in the future of a relationship with someone who is more rather than less similar to them. Finally, it may be that it is not just similarity in demographics or attitudes or whatever that directly influences interpersonal attraction, but also the similarity in emotional responses thereby generated. In other words, people who are similar in a variety of ways may respond to various situations in an emotionally congruent manner and therefore be more likely to be attracted to each other.

Sometimes, similarity of attitudes can matter in a rather perverse way. For example, it has been found that individuals who possess negative self-concepts, or images of themselves, tend to be more committed to marital partners who evaluate them negatively than to partners who evaluate them positively. In contrast, people with positive self-concepts prefer to stay with those who evaluate them positively.[38] The somewhat depressing conclusion of this research is that, if you are trying to bolster someone with a low self-concept, they are likely to dump you before they dump their negative self-concept!

Barriers

One of the longest-running and most successful of off-Broadway plays is *Fantasticks*. The play is about a boy and a girl whose fathers are sworn enemies and have, as a result, erected a high wall separating their properties. The boy and girl come to know each other, fall in love, and go to great lengths to see each other in secret trysts. The fathers, upon discovering the relationship between their children, discourage them but eventually come to the conclusion that they will not be able to prevent the relationship. Hence, they tear down the wall. But as soon as they tear down the wall, problems emerge. What once had been an intimate and harmonious relationship becomes more distant and discordant. Eventually, the boy goes off to see the world; the girl, left behind, also gets to see what else is around. After many trials and tribulations, the boy and the girl are reunited. But now the fathers, having learned a lesson, rebuild the wall in order to create an obstacle separating the two. The lesson they have learned is that love seems to flourish only in the face of obstacles.

The theme of *Fantasticks* is actually supported by psychological research. For example, parental interference in a relationship tends to bring the partners in it closer together. If parents want to discourage an intimate relationship, the worst thing they can do is actively to interfere with it.[39]

Couples sometimes achieve intimacy by creating outside enemies who are out to get them. The enemies may be friends, parents-in-law, stepchildren, or, for that matter, the government. Sometimes, of course, one's perception of these external enemies is not paranoid but realistic: Sometimes people or government agencies really are out to get a couple. But it is useful to have an external enemy – so long as it is relatively impotent. Enemy seeking has its drawbacks: Couples who get in the habit risk eventually finding the enemy in one another.

In conclusion, unless at least some of the factors in interpersonal attraction – physical attractiveness, arousal, proximity, reciprocity, similarity, and barriers – are operating for a couple, it is unlikely that they will reach the point of falling in love. What are some theories of how these and other variables operate?

THEORIES OF ATTRACTION

The Hard-to-Get Theory

One of the most common observations in everyday life – that people want what they cannot have – holds for relationships, too: one is attracted to the man or woman who is "hard to get." But it is not quite that simple. People tend to be attracted not to those who are hard to get, in general, but to those who are hard for *others* to get but relatively easier to get for themselves.[40]

There is, though, an irony in all this. After basking in the glory of being "unique," some of these people come to feel their freedom being threatened and to worry about being rushed into a commitment. They begin to withdraw, and the relationship ends. What works in the short term may backfire in the long term.

In the psychological literature, *reactance theory* seeks to explain why some people want what they have difficulty getting.[41] In effect, they react against perceived threats to their freedom of choice. According to this theory, people tend to rebel when their freedom of choice is taken away from them – that is, they react against the restriction of their freedom. Thus, things you may once not have wanted when they were readily available to you, you may want after they are no longer available to you.

Reactance theory has an interesting implication for why couples who live together before marriage are no more likely to stay together after marriage than are couples who do not first live together. In Sweden, at least, such couples actually are more likely later to divorce. When a couple lives together without marriage, there may be ties of all kinds, but each member of the couple knows that the other could walk out, legally, at any time and without any notice. There may be psychological commitments, but there is no legal one; and either member of the couple who dispenses with the psychological commitment is always free to leave. Marriage can generate a state of reactance, especially among those who are used to their freedom, and it is likely that those who choose to live together without marriage may be particularly concerned with retaining some additional sense of autonomy.

Because of the lack of a formal commitment in living together, one is susceptible to relying more on what a partner can do for one than on what one can do for a partner.[42] Such a "consumer" orientation to relationships is bound to lead to repeated disappointments, making it impossible to sustain a strong and mutually supportive reciprocal intimate relationship. You need to find someone who not only has a lot to offer you, but also stands to benefit unusually well from what you have to give, and whose receipt of it makes you feel good about the relationship and about yourself.

Several theories have been developed about how people select particular partners: similarity, complementarity, sequential filtering, stimulus-value-role, and dyadic formation.

Similarity Theory

Until recently, the received view was that people select mates who are similar to themselves. Indeed, similarity is an important variable in attraction and intimacy, as discussed earlier. According to the similarity view, we tend to select as mates people who reward us, and probably the single most rewarding aspect of a potential mate is similarity to oneself.[43] It is obvious that people look for others similar to themselves in at least some fundamental ways, but theorists who talk merely about similarity often do not make clear the ways in which we want a partner to be similar or different. One group of theorists particularly concerned with this issue has investigated complementarity.

Complementarity Theory

Some theorists have suggested that we look for people as mates primarily not because they are *similar* to us, but rather because they are *complementary* to us: That is, they excel in or do something we do not excel in or do.[44] Thus, if you don't like doing dishes or cleaning house, you might want a mate who would do these things. If you don't like handling finances, it would make good sense to find someone who does. If you talk a lot, then you might want to find somebody who listens.

The evidence in favor of complementarity theory is mixed. For example, you would probably expect that couples would work best when one member is masculine in orientation and the other is feminine in orientation, an obvious complementarity. In fact, what seems obvious in this case turns out not to be true. Relationship satisfaction for both men and women is associated with a feminine orientation on the part of both partners, where such an orientation is defined in terms of expressivity of emotions and thoughts.[45] Along these lines, people tend to be more attractive if they are more disclosing in an intimate relationship.[46] However, inappropriate self-disclosure does not work. People tend to avoid those who go into their life story at the first available opportunity.[47]

Thus, femininity in terms of disclosure and expression tends to be associated with success in relationships. In fact, the traditional sex-role couple tends to have the lowest satisfaction of the various possible pairings that have been studied.[48]

Although complementarity does not always work, there is one respect in which it is clear that complementarity is a plus. Researchers have found that when a partner's performance surpasses one's own on a dimension highly relevant to one's self-concept, one's self-esteem is likely to be threatened, and one's attraction to the partner is likely to be decreased. In contrast, when a partner's performance surpasses one's own on a dimension that is not highly relevant to one's self-concept, one's self-esteem is not threatened, and one's attraction for the partner is likely actually to increase.[49]

Sequential Filtering Theory

It would seem reasonable to combine the similarity and complementarity points of view, which is what sequential filtering theory does.[50] According to this theory, one first looks for people who are similar to oneself in the basics, such as social class, religion, race, upbringing, and so on. If one continues in a relationship, and begins to view the partner as a potential mate, one seeks similarity also in personal values. Finally, complementarity begins to play a role in the course of the relationship over a somewhat longer time. According to this theory, one is likely to value and stay in a relationship if a potential mate also fills one's needs.

Although the model is attractive, support for it is mixed.[51] A study testing this model found that a better predictor of relationship progress was the couple's prediction of what its progress would be over time. Thus, what a couple thought would happen was a better predictor of what would actually happen than was either value consensus or need complementarity.

Stimulus-Value-Role Theory

According to the stimulus-value-role theory of mate selection, in order for two people to be attracted to one another, they need initially to respond to each other on a basic, simple level – physical appearance, financial position, religious or ethnic background, style of dress, first impression of personality, and the like.[52] Basically, one gets together with people whose assets and liabilities, or strengths and weaknesses, seem to provide a likely match to oneself.

When people do get together, then values start to become more important. A relationship is likely to continue on the road to a committed permanent union if, at a deeper level, one finds that one shares personal, family, and generalized values with the other person. Important here are such values as views about having and raising children, the importance of religion in life, earning and spending money, time spent on work versus time spent on play, and so on. Even if one is initially attracted to someone, the relationship is unlikely to forge ahead unless, in the second stage, the partners can achieve some degree of value consensus. If they cannot, they are likely to view the relationship as superficial, and to seek other, more compatible partners.

In the third and last stage, which continues the filtering process whereby one weeds out people not compatible with oneself, role issues become important. Can one find, in the day-to-day functioning of the relationship, complementary roles such that one feels comfortable interacting with the other person? Here arise such issues as allocation of labor: who takes care of the house, the finances, the social life of the couple, and so on. One can have values similar to those of another person but find that one's role expectations for oneself and the other do not coincide. In other words, there may be some roles that both partners want and other roles that neither wants. Unless they can work out division of labor and allocation of responsibility, the relationship is unlikely to continue or, if it does, to succeed.

Theory of Dyadic Formation

Another theory suggests that early processes in a relationship need to be successfully completed before moving on to later ones.[53] The six processes on the proposed list are perceiving similarities, achieving pair rapport, attaining openness in communication through mutual self-disclosure, achieving comfortable roles for each person, achieving roles that are comfortable for the other as well as for oneself, and attaining so-called dyadic crystallization, whereby commitment to each other and identity as a couple are established.

The theories we have considered have derived primarily from social psychology. A second group of theories has derived more from the experiences of clinicians who work with individuals in psychotherapeutic practice.

Clinical Theories

Freud. Sigmund Freud viewed love in terms of sublimated sexuality.[54] Because we want sexual relations more frequently, with more people, and in more places than society in general or other people in particular will allow, love is a way of sublimating – bringing to a higher plain – our unacceptable sexual desires. It rechannels at least some of these desires in a socially acceptable way.

Adult love also helps to rechannel the frustration stemming from childhood when boys and girls are disappointed to find that their desire for and passion toward the parent of the opposite sex (the Oedipus and the Electra complexes, respectively) cannot be fulfilled. After this painful discovery, which usually occurs around the age of six, children enter a latency period, in which their desire for a member of the opposite sex becomes dormant. Hurt by the perceived rejection by the opposite-sex parent, the child simply represses all his or her sexual desires. During the latency period, many boys want to have as little to do with girls as possible, and vice versa.

Reik. Theodore Reik, on the other hand, viewed love as arising out of dissatisfaction with oneself and one's lot in life.[55] People seek out love and especially passion when life is disappointing and when they need someone else to fill the void within. Some people seek salvation in love, much as other people do in religion, hoping to find in another the perfection they cannot find in themselves. At first, they may well think that salvation is at hand. Early in a relationship, their partner may indeed seem to be just what they are looking for, and their being in love is tantamount to being saved – from the world and often from themselves. But eventually disillusionment is almost certain to set in. They discover two facts. First, the other person has flaws: They cannot maintain the illusion of perfection in the face of ever more evidence that the partner is not, in fact, perfect. Second, no other human can save them, not even the love of their life.

Perhaps one can save oneself, but one cannot expect or even ask this of another. People have either to adjust to a new kind of love or else forever live with the disappointment of knowing that they cannot find salvation through love of another. Of course, some people take a third course: They try to find someone else to save them and once again reenter the cycle of high hopes followed by disappointment.

While, on the one hand, people may know at an intellectual level that no one can "save" another through love, they may, on the other hand, find it hard to convince themselves of it at an emotional level.

Klein. According to Melanie Klein, who holds a view related to Reik's, love arises from one's dependency upon others for the satisfaction of one's needs.[56] Some degree of dependence is healthy, and people who cannot allow themselves to be at all dependent are likely to be unhappy.

Maslow. Abraham Maslow's "D-love," or "deficiency love," is also of the kind noted by Reik and Klein, arising from the need for security and belonging.[57] Indeed, the term *deficiency* provides an apt characterization of most of these theories, in that they view love as arising from some lack or feeling of something missing within the person. Maslow's "B-love," or "being love," arises out of a person's higher emotional needs, especially the desire for self-actualization and actualization of another.[58] This kind of love represents for Maslow the highest kind of personal fulfillment. D-love appears to be more passion driven, B-love, more intimacy driven.

Psychological theories are products of their time. Thus, Sigmund Freud's theory is often thought to reflect the Victorian times of which he was a product; and Maslow's seems to be a good match to the 1960s, the "me era," during which self-actualization was seen by many as the attainment of the highest level of emotional well-being. Reading Maslow on being love, one may wonder whether any couple has ever had the kind of completely secure, placid, and untroubled love he describes. Perhaps not. Anyone who did have it would quickly become bored. Full self-actualization for oneself and another may be a fine goal, but most of the pleasure may be in getting there; anyone who ever reached the tranquil, self-sufficient state Maslow describes might end up generating problems to stir things up.

Fromm. Erich Fromm, living in roughly the same era as Maslow, viewed love as arising from care, responsibility, respect, and knowledge of another.[59] The sources of Fromm's theory are clear: Fromm was caught up in and much affected by the fascist madness in the Second World War. For him, love was an escape from that madness; caring, responsibility, respect, and trust all seemed to be missing from that world.

Lee. John Lee has used the metaphor of colors as the basis for his proposal for a typology of kinds of love that may attract us.[60] One could imagine different kinds of love arrayed in a wheel, just like the color wheel. Lee derived the typology not only from the metaphor but from an examination of literature, both fiction and nonfiction, which he then verified on the basis of a large study.

Lee's typology distinguishes among six major kinds of love:

1. *Eros:* the love style characterized by the search for a beloved whose physical presentation of self embodies an image already held in the mind of the lover.
2. *Ludus:* Ovid's term for playful or gamelike love.
3. *Storge:* an intimate style based on slowly developing affection and companionship.

4. *Mania:* a passionate love style characterized by obsession, jealousy, and great emotional intensity.
5. *Agape:* altruistic love, in which the lover views it as his or her duty to love without expectation of reciprocation.
6. *Pragma:* a practical style involving conscious consideration of the demographic and other objective characteristics of the loved one.

Marcia Lasswell and Norman Lobsenz used Lee's theory as the basis for their construction of the Love Scale Questionnaire.[61] Some of the strongest validation for Lee's theory has come from recent work of Clyde Hendrick and Susan Hendrick, who have tested the metaphor with their own questionnaire, using factor-analytic methods.[62]

A given person does not necessarily display the same style in each of his or her relationships. Rather, different relationships may evoke different styles of loving. Moreover, people may switch from one style to another over time within a single relationship. It is useful to know and understand both your own and your partner's style of loving within a given relationship. For example, a ludic lover may well be playing the field while going out with you and "forget" to mention it, whereas the manic lover is much less likely to play the field but may well explode if you do. The storgic lover may develop into your best friend but is less likely to develop into your most intense romance. Such a romance is much more likely with an erotic lover. And if you become involved with an agapic lover, do not expect always to be at the center of his or her attention: The person who loves agapically tends to be very giving – and may well give of his or her selflessness to others beside yourself. Finally, if yours is a pragmatic lover, be prepared for a relationship based on practicalities that may even smack at times of a business deal.

Whomever we are attracted to, attraction can be sufficient to start a relationship, but it is not sufficient to keep it going. In Part IV, we consider what keeps relationships going once they have gotten off the ground. We start in Chapter 10 with one of the most important mechanisms for the sustenance of a relationship, reward.

Cupid's Arrow in Flight: Love in Our Lifetime: Middles

10

The Role of Reward

Suppose you are introduced to someone who immediately compliments you on something that matters to you: It might be your looks, or your brains, or your brawn, or whatever. Chances are you will like that person the more for the compliment. After all, the person has rewarded you. In psychological terms, you have been reinforced by the person, who has increased your intimacy toward and attraction to him or her. The compliment probably won't excite great passion that you weren't already feeling, but it may well increase feelings of intimacy – the feeling that this is someone you'd like to get to know and to talk to further.

Unfortunately, there is a flip side to reinforcement – punishment. People in relationships sometimes act in ways to hurt each other. Those actions, whether intentional or wholly inadvertent, increase your aversion to the person. The sad part is that the aversion may not go away, even after you forgive the person (if you do!). Most reinforcements and punishments in interpersonal relationships provoke emotional responses over which one has relatively little conscious control. One wishes to decrease intimacy or, in the extreme, have as little to do with the person as possible. For example, seeing someone who hurt you in the past may evoke a feeling of wanting to stay away from the person, even though you may not want to have that feeling.

For example, Jill went through a bitter divorce from her husband, Bill, who acted cruelly during the proceeding. For him, divorce meant getting the most you could for yourself, even at the other person's expense. After it was all over, Bill wanted to let bygones be bygones and to be friends with Jill. But although she could forgive him, she couldn't forget. Every time she saw him, she felt a knot starting to form in her stomach. Bill couldn't understand that the very sight of him had become a punishment to Jill, a punishment that Jill now tried to avoid at all costs.

REINFORCEMENT THEORY

Though it sometimes oversimplifies a situation, reinforcement theory often provides the simplest and most elegant explanation of what goes on in interpersonal relationships. The basic principles of reinforcement, while apparently obvious, actually have nonobvious implications. A person who has a low opinion of herself, for example, will find beliefs that concur with her own to be reinforcing. Ironically, she may be most reinforced when someone expresses a low rather than a high opinion of her, because the low opinion concurs with hers.

Consider a second implication of reinforcement theory – a powerful one for why things can go wrong in a relationship. We know that, on average, people react more strongly to negative comments than to positive ones. In letters of recommendation, for example, negative comments generally carry far more weight than do positive ones. In relationships, too, punishments often carry more weight than do rewards. Over time, then, your partner can come to have more ability to punish you than to reinforce you positively. The buildup of negatives may therefore come to exceed the buildup of positives, and a relationship may seem less and less attractive over time, just because the buildup of punishments over time is having more of an effect than the buildup of rewards. The experience of intimacy is on the way down.

According to reinforcement theory, liking for a person will result when one experiences reward in the presence of that person.[1] An implication of this view is that you can come to like someone not because of who the person is, but because you happen to experience positive reinforcements in his or her presence. Similarly, you can come to dislike people who are associated with unpleasant circumstances. Research has shown that one comes to like people who only incidentally are associated with positive reinforcement.[2] For example, children who were systematically rewarded by their teacher came to like their class-mates more than did children who were either ignored or punished by their teacher.

On the opposite side of the coin, people tend to dislike strangers whom they meet in a hot, crowded room, regardless of their actual personalities.[3] This principle shows why it is a mistake, in relationships, to keep putting off for tomorrow (or the next day or the next) the fun you could have today. It is very easy to put a relationship on the back burner while you attend to other things. The problem is that if you and your partner don't do things that you enjoy, there is no fun to rub off onto the relationship. In fact, if you do little together, or do mostly things that are boring, you can quickly find yourself bored with each other.

A fairly typical professional couple, Louis and Ann, are both concerned about their professional advancement. They understand each other in this regard, because they both want the same thing – to come out on top in their work. It always seems that if one of them is not temporarily snowed under by work, the other is. They rarely have time to do things together, but have been expecting – for half a decade – that the "busy time will pass."

By now they seem to have forgotten how to have fun together and enjoy each other, and are obviously using their work to avoid the fact that their relationship has become a sad example of empty love. They are a good example of how the process can change the product. They once saw professional advancement for each of them as their mutual goal to happiness. But their absorption in the professional domain left them with little in the personal domain, and now they seem unable to recover what they lost. Intimacy started to flag and, with it, passion and commitment.

A potent source of intimacy is attitudinal similarity.[4] Why? Attitudinal similarity may lead to intimacy because it provides one with independent evidence for the correctness and value of one's opinions. You can talk to someone who shares your opinions, but it is often harder to achieve intimacy with someone who disagrees with you at every turn.

What does all this mean in practical terms? For one thing, it helps explain why newcomers can threaten old relationships. When you have known someone for a long time, you are likely to know many of their attitudes, and, almost inevitably, there will be a fair number that you do not share. In the case of someone you have just met, you will learn initially only a few of that person's attitudes: It takes a while to learn any substantial number of them.

If, initially, a few of the other person's attitudes are inconsistent with your own, you are likely to be rapidly turned off, even though these attitudes are only a small portion of the person's entire set of attitudes. Suppose in meeting a new person, however, you find you agree with the attitudes you learn about initially. Although the number of agreements may be small, because you don't yet know much about the new person, the proportion of agreements will be high.

Voila! You are attracted: You feel a sense of budding intimacy. The new attraction may not last, however. If the initial attitudes you learn about are mostly ones you agree with, there is a good chance you are getting a biased sample and that, as you get to know more of that person's attitudes, the disagreements will be greater than you thought.

Of course, many different kinds of things can be positively reinforcing. One psychologist suggests that there are three major categories of reward: intrinsic characteristics of a person, such as beauty, sense of humor, and intelligence; behavior of the person toward one, such as providing sexual attention or consolation in times of stress; and access to desired external resources granted by the other person, such as prestige, money, and other people.[5]

People often make one or both of two wrong assumptions in relationships. These assumptions lead to frustration and often to dissatisfaction.

The first wrong assumption is that the other person values what they do: If they think love is important, they assume the other person does too; or if they think money is important, they assume the other does as well. In truth, we are usually better off assuming nothing. Find out what the other person values. Ask the person, and also watch what kinds of reward (and punishment) he or she most responds to.

The second wrong assumption is that the other person does – or should – value what they have a lot of. Especially when people travel outside their own immediate circle of friends and colleagues, they may find that other people don't respond, because their values are different from the anticipated ones.

In my first talk to a group of business executives, my introducer went through a long string of academic credentials. Looking at those in the audience, I could see that I had lost them before I had even started. Not only did they not pay much attention to the talk, but after it, no one seemed much interested in getting to know me personally.

Their assumption was that no one of any real interest could come from inside the "ivory tower." Not only did they not value the credentials, but they were suspicious of them. It would be like introducing someone to a lover of the environment for a potential romance and mentioning during the introduction that the potential partner represents industries in their fight against rabid crazed environmentalists who can think of nothing except a few trees and animals.

This principle applies in many different situations. You have to know what reinforces a person and thus will cause him or her to pursue intimacy. Consider an ill-fated introduction observed at a dinner party.

A man was trying to impress a woman with hints of his financial well-being. He seemed impressed with himself, but she certainly was not impressed with him. She promptly excused herself and would not talk to him for the rest of the evening. The man made the mistake of assuming the woman valued what he did, rather than first finding out what she did, in fact, value – which was the overthrow of a value system that puts such a high premium on financial success.

SOCIAL-EXCHANGE THEORY

Social-exchange theory is a more specific form of reinforcement theory, as applied to personal relationships. According to social exchange theory, people seek to maximize rewards and minimize punishments.[6] People will therefore feel greater intimacy and more attraction toward those who provide more rewards and fewer punishments. But there are limits on the reward value of any kind of resource. Imelda Marcos probably found that, after the first few hundred pairs of shoes she owned, any one subsequent pair brought her less happiness than did the first few new pairs.

At work here is the learning principle of satiation, which holds that the more of something a person has, the less valuable further increases in it will be. Just as a thousand dollars means less to a millionaire than to a pauper, being liked by someone is less valuable to a person who is almost universally well liked than to a person who is generally not well liked.

The economic principle of supply and demand also applies to social relationships: People are willing to pay more for scarce resources than for abundant ones. Hence, one may be more willing to give up a lot to obtain the attentions of another if that person is unique in the attentions or resources he or she has to offer than if those attentions or resources are readily available from others.

Social-exchange theory has several important implications for interpersonal relationships. These principles can be invaluable to those who are seeking intimacy with others.

A first principle is that people want most to be rewarded in their areas of insecurity. Jane, for example, is a professional woman, who is forever being complimented on her looks. As a result, the man to whom she is most likely to respond is not the one who compliments her on her appearance but the one who instead compliments her on her professional work, an arena in which she feels insecure.

The insecurity does not necessarily have any basis in facts. For example, Jane may actually be relatively more competent in her work than she is attractive, but men may think that she wants to hear that she is attractive. What matters is not how good she or anyone else really is in any objective sense, but how she or anyone else feels about herself (or himself).

A second implication of social-exchange theory may be summed up in the old adage that, in the country of the blind, the one-eyed man is king. The underlying principle is that what matters is not what you do well, but what you do well that others don't do as well.

When in a competitive situation, whether at work or in personal life, people tend to stress what they are good at. Social-exchange theory points out that this stress isn't quite right. What one needs to stress is what one is particularly good at that others are not. In other words, what distinguishes you from the rest?

George, a doctor seeking a romantic partner, uses this principle very well. When he meets someone at a party of doctors, he doesn't even bother to play up his medical expertise. His view – right or wrong – is first that the women he meets will assume that all the doctors at a gathering are good, and that any differences will be insignificant to them, however significant they may be to other doctors; and, second, that women who meet doctors are concerned more about their being tight-fisted, egotistical, and possibly "workaholic" than about their being professionally competent. George, therefore, stresses his personal qualities – what he thinks will set him apart from other men in the minds of the women he meets.

At times, one has to face the issue of people to whom one might be attracted but who just don't value what one has to offer. For example, Martha also goes to many parties of doctors, not because she anticipates meeting a doctor but because she is a doctor herself who is looking to meet someone. Her interactions with men have often been disappointing to her, because she has found that, to her consternation, her being a doctor is often viewed as a negative rather than as a plus. The men she meets seem interested in the resources she may bring to the marriage, but at the same time they seem turned off by someone they view as professionally very successful and potentially threatening to their egos. The more they learn about her successes, the less interested they seem!

Martha went through a period of trying to hide her success so as to maintain the interest of the men she was meeting. Eventually, though, she decided that this path was not the right one for her to be taking – that she had to find someone who, rather than running away, would appreciate her for her accomplishments. Her move is a good one, because she would be wasting her time establishing a relationship under false pretenses with someone who doesn't appreciate her for the person she is and the accomplishments she has realized. In particular, she needs someone who feels like he will be gaining a more attractive person because of her success, not losing an attractive person. In short, she needs someone with whom she can establish equity.

EQUITY THEORY

Equity theory can be understood in terms of just four propositions.[7] These propositions all derive from the notion that we are happiest in relationships in which what we give is proportionate to what we receive.

First, individuals try to maximize their outcomes (that is, the rewards minus the punishments received). No surprise there. People basically want the best for themselves they can get.

Second, partners can maximize their collective reward by developing an agreed-upon system for fairly apportioning available rewards and costs between themselves. If one partner likes to go to movies and the other likes to go to concerts, the couple will be happiest if each gets his or her own way about half the time.

Third, when people find themselves in an inequitable relationship, they become distressed. The amount of distress is proportional to the inequity experienced. If the couple always goes to the movies or always goes to the concerts, one or the other of the partners is going to be unhappy.

Finally, people will attempt to eliminate the distress they are experiencing by restoring equity to the relationship: The greater the experienced inequity, the greater the effort to restore equity. The partner who is being shortchanged on the entertainment is likely to take steps of one kind or another to change things.

People will be more attracted to and feel greater intimacy toward those with whom they have a more equitable relationship. They are attracted to people who take in proportion to what they give. People who are selfish may get their way in a close relationship, but often at the cost of intimacy in the relationship. The relationship may last, but often in name only; the feelings of warmth, sharing, and closeness are not likely to last with it.

Equity theory has an interesting implication for those who have felt victimized by someone in the past. The implication is relevant to victims who cannot or will not terminate a relationship with someone who has exploited them. It is that the victims will tend to fare better if, in communicating with the person who has hurt or exploited them, they minimize the amount of harm they say they have endured. Otherwise, the exploiter may conclude that the victim has endured so much harm that equity cannot possibly be restored. The exploiter may then convince himself or herself that the victims actually deserved the harm that was done to them.

Exploited groups, of course, are often made to feel as though they deserve the treatment they are getting – a surprising implication of equity theory. In order to "restore" equity, the aggressors convince themselves that the exploited groups are, in fact, being treated equitably.

Nelson Mandela, as president of South Africa, forgave people who imprisoned him for most of his adult life. His forgiveness may well have derived from generosity of spirit or from Christian principles. But his forgiveness also made sense in terms of equity theory. Mandela had the wisdom to realize that there was no other viable option to heal his nation.

The Tutsi-controlled government of Rwanda has faced the same test. The Tutsis and the Hutus in Rwanda had a history of living together, much as did the Serbs, Croats, and Bosnians in the former Yugoslavia. But then a government bent on genocide fomented divisions among groups, leading to a massacre of the Tutsis by the Hutus. As usually happens, atrocities came to be committed on both sides. Eventually, the Tutsis overthrew the Hutu government. Many Hutus fled elsewhere, where they were not welcomed. The Tutsi government would then presumably be best off trying to incorporate them back into the country, realizing that the only other option – continued warfare and genocide – would be far less desirable.

Equity theory has important implications for all our relationships and especially our intimate ones. The first and simplest implication is that, over the long term, it is important that both members of a couple feel that their rewards (and punishments) from the relationship are approximately equal. Over the short term, there will always be inequities – one person, for example, making sacrifices for the sake of the other's work. But what starts to destroy a relationship is when it is always the same person making the sacrifices.

Sometimes one member of the couple may think that his or her career or other interests are the more important. The two members of the couple may even agree on this decision, for financial or other reasons. But if the one who makes the sacrifices for the other's career is not recompensed in some other way, the debts will build up, and sooner or later both members of the couple will pay.

Tanya and Bernardo have managed to work out a reasonably creative solution to the problem of career moves. Bernardo is in a large, high-tech firm that tends to transfer its employees a lot. The couple's agreement is that they move to another locale for Bernardo, but Tanya gets her pick of house and neighborhood. Each has veto power, so that if Tanya absolutely does not want to move again, they don't move; and if Bernardo can't stand the house or the neighborhood, they look for something else. Neither has ever used the veto power, but having it gives each of them a safety valve that seems necessary for the relationship to keep working.

Another implication of equity theory is that when you feel wronged by your partner, continually throwing that wrong in the partner's face is likely to backfire. The partner who feels that no matter what he or she does, equity cannot be restored, may decide to give up on the whole thing.

Eric and Davida had been married for seven years when Davida had an affair. Eric found out. The affair had been just a fling, but Eric used it as a weapon, bringing it up every time he and Davida had a fight. After a while, Eric brought it up any time he wanted to make a point with Davida. Davida tried – unsuccessfully – to get him to stop. It was getting old, fast. He wouldn't cut it out. She eventually left him, feeling unable to restore equity, no matter what she did. Now Eric has lost both his bargaining chip and his wife.

What leads some relationships, like Eric's and Davida's, to fall apart, and others to follow a better course? We consider this issue in Chapter 11.

11

The Course
of Relationships

If you were solicited for a major financial investment that was likely to
pay off just over 50 percent of the time, or asked to play Russian
roulette with the same probability of not being killed, chances are that
you would neither make the investment nor play the game. Yet people
routinely enter into marriages with roughly the same probability of
success. Few people start out expecting to become victims of divorce,
any more than smokers expect to become victims of lung cancer or Cal-
ifornians of earthquake. Yet, if the divorce rate remains constant, close
to half of the men and women currently entering into marriages can
expect eventually to divorce.

Perhaps many intimate relationships, including marriages, terminate
because people make poor decisions about a potential partner: They
misevaluate the evidence or do not seek the most useful evidence in the
first place. Another explanation, the focus of this chapter, is not that
people pick the wrong partners, but that they select partners on the basis of what matters early in an intimate relationship rather than what
might matter over the long run. And, of course, intimate relationships
and the people in them change over time in ways that are not fully predictable to begin with. In this chapter, I discuss studies of changes in
relationships.

RELATIONSHIP DEVELOPMENT

Relationships develop through a process of social penetration. *Social penetration* refers both to external behavior and to internal feelings that precede, accompany, and follow behavior.[1] Basically, according to this theory, our interactions with others have two aspects: breadth and depth. *Breadth* refers to the range of topics we discuss and to the interactions we have. *Depth* refers to the level at which we discuss and interact on each of these topics. Relationships vary in terms of the breadth and depth of social penetration. For example, with someone who is merely an acquaintance, one's interactions will be on a limited number of topics at a superficial depth. In a casual friendship, one may interact on more topics but still not get to their core. In a deeper friendship or the beginning of an intimate relationship, the range of topics continues to expand at the same time that we begin to discuss them deeply. Finally, relationships that become truly intimate increase further in both breadth and depth. In other words, the partners begin to share all of themselves, interacting on all topics, those not only in the present but also in areas of concern from their past and for their future. They discuss these topics in greater detail and with great feeling. The extent of breadth and depth indicates the degree of social penetration.

Not all relationships proceed breadth-first. Occasionally, one may have an intense interaction with another, but only in a limited range of topics. The "stranger on the train" phenomenon, whereby one spills out some aspect of one's life story to a person one has met casually and expects never to see again, is an example of a relationship in which considerable depth may be achieved for only a few topics. Or one may have a friendship with a particular person in which one bares one's soul, but probably in only a specific area of concern that happens to be at the forefront of one's mind at the moment and needs to be vented.

STUDIES OF RELATIONSHIP CHANGE

Social penetration and the development of relationships have been investigated in many studies. One study involved a follow-up of 182 couples six months after an initial questionnaire session.[2] Slightly more than 80 percent of the couples were still together; 60 percent of couples reported that their relationships had become more intense, 19 percent reported no change in intensity, and 21 percent reported a decrease in intensity. Most of the couples in the last category had broken up. The relationships most likely to have broken up were those that had lasted either for the shortest or the longest time. Apparently, the shortest-termers in the original study were still unstable, and the longest-termer were susceptible to being in relationships that were coming close to having run their course.

Scores on a love scale predicted favorable progress in the relationships to only a slight degree.[3] But the correlations of love-scale scores and progress in relationships were higher for those individuals who had indicated, in the initial study, that they lived in accordance with more romantic ideals, as captured by such statements as "A person should marry whomever he loves regardless of social position" and "As long as they at least love one another, two people should have no difficulty getting along together in marriage." For couples in which both partners were romantic, the correlations between initial love-scale scores and progress six months later were moderate, somewhat higher for men than for women. Correlations for a liking scale were in the same direction, but weaker.

This study helps explain why some seemingly loveless relationships engender commitment and can go on and on, whereas others terminate rapidly. Most of us know couples who stay together in what seem to be dead relationships (at least emotionally), and other couples who break up as soon as one member of the couple stops feeling "in love." The critical issue is the perception of each member of the couple regarding how important love, and especially romantic love, is for the survival of a relationship. An additional variable affecting the equation is what the members of a couple expect not just for relationships in general but for a given relationship in particular. Some people, for example, adore erotic relationships but do not expect a marriage to survive as this kind of relationship over the long term.

The biggest problem, and a frequent one, is when each member of a couple has a different perception either of the importance of love in a relationship or of what love means in their relationship. Cathy and

George provide a case in point. After being married for over a decade, they appeared to have everything; a nice house, two successful careers, four wonderful children, lots of discretionary money to spend, status in the community, and practically anything else a couple could want. The problem was that Cathy was unhappy, but George was not. Cathy felt she had everything and yet nothing. However great her life looked, it was empty except for her love of her four children and their love of her. What love she may have once had for George had given way to what she referred to as "patience." She tolerated him but found herself emotionally disengaged. She felt that there had to be more to life, and love, than this. She was considering giving up on the marriage, and the nice house and the money and the picture-perfect environment she lived in, to seek a man whom she could feel really crazy about.

George felt that Cathy would be crazy to give up what they had because they had it all. And George was right – for George. His notion of love was much more placid than Cathy's. Passionate feelings were not important to him in a marriage, and he was comfortable with modest amounts of intimacy. He and Cathy had a commitment to each other, and that commitment had brought them all they wanted, and more. But the lack of passion and intimacy in the relationship was increasingly frustrating to Cathy, and she didn't know what to do about it. She was still deciding at last count, as she had been for the past five years, and might well be for another five or more.

Unfortunately, there is no one right answer to Cathy's problem, because it involves so many factors. She will have to take into account not only her feelings for George, or the lack thereof, but also the emotional needs of the children, financial security, effects on living arrangements, and so on. It is not surprising that she, like many others in her position, finds herself in a state of prolonged indecision.

The study described earlier examined relationships over the course of only six months. Another study looked at 103 relationships that broke up over a period of two years.[4] The researchers examined factors that predict termination of intimate relationships among college students prior to marriage and found that unequal involvement in a relationship, as well as discrepancies in age, educational aspirations, intelligence, and physical attractiveness, were predictive of breakups. The timing of breakups was closely related to the school calendar: They tended to occur at the natural beginnings and ends of school terms. The decision to terminate a relationship was seldom mutual, and women were more likely than men both to perceive problems in a relationship and to make the decision to terminate it.

This study affirms the importance of similarity and reciprocity in relationships. It also illustrates how dissimilarities that may not be problematical over the short term can become so over the long term. Consider, for example, unequal involvement. Early on, a person may be flattered (and even floored) by the high level of involvement another exhibits toward him or her. And if the person has felt relatively unloved for a long time, the interest of the other may be especially welcome. The person may feel less toward the other but be so grateful for the love received that he or she is content to be the more loved partner.

Stacey was in just this position. At twenty-five, she had been in few relationships, none of which had lasted long, and was starting to panic. She had recently heard of a study that supposedly showed that her chances of marrying were already becoming remote, and she really wanted to have children as well as a good relationship. When Charles, whom she had recently met, declared his love for her, she was almost ecstatic, despite the fact that she did not feel much for him. She stayed with him for over a year and then left the relationship. She had hoped to "learn to love" Charles, but never did. Moreover, she had become frustrated being in a relationship that was grossly asymmetrical. She now felt suffocated by Charles's love, probably because she was unable to reciprocate it.

An age difference can also be an unpredictable factor in a loving relationship. The most common difference, of course, is for the man to be older than the woman. When the difference is large, problems may result over the long term. Lydia was delighted with Joe on first meeting: She was twenty-three, and he was forty-nine. Lydia, who had had a troubled relationship with her father, was looking for the father figure she never had. Joe was it. Within a year after meeting, Joe and Lydia were married. By the age of thirty, Lydia no longer needed or wanted a father figure. She had worked through her early troubled relationship with her father, largely with Joe's help. Joe, at fifty-six, was viewing his life as winding down, while Lydia was looking now to start winding her life up. The couple encountered serious difficulties, which eventually they worked through. Joe and Lydia saw a counselor and realized that part of their problem was not in their objective age difference but in Joe's perception of himself at fifty-six as ready to wind down. His psychological rather than biological age was the problem. As Joe began to realize that he need not be an old man at fifty-six, he was able to rally to save a marriage that meant a lot to him.

Differences in education and educational aspirations can also affect the well-being of a marriage. Don married a woman while she was an undergraduate and he a medical student about to get his degree. Sally dropped out of school but told Don she later wanted to go back, finish, and have a career. Don didn't take what she said seriously, because a lot of women seemed to be talking that way at the time – maybe, he thought, to save face. Most of them, he believed, ultimately settled down, had children, and provided the kind of tranquil, stable family life he wanted while he pursued his career as a doctor. Don later discovered that Sally was totally serious in her educational aspirations, so serious that she wanted to finish school before having children. She did – minus Don, who was last heard of looking for another wife to be the docile homebody he wanted.

As for intelligence, almost everyone seems to be looking for an intelligent partner these days. A match in intelligence makes sense in that someone who is very intelligent may become bored with someone who is distinctly lacking in intelligence. But intelligence takes many forms, not all of them measurable by academic honors or other clear signs. One can be seriously misled by equating a potential partner's success or failure in school with his or her intellectual prowess and compatibility.

CLUSTERS OF CHARACTERISTICS THAT MATTER OVER TIME

In one of our own cross-sectional studies, which addressed what matters when in a relationship, we identified ten major clusters that matter to relationships over time.[5] Subjects were eighty New Haven area adults ranging in age from seventeen to sixty-nine years, with a mean of thirty-one years. In descending order of importance, they are intimate communication/support, understanding/appreciation, tolerance/ acceptance, flexibility/modifiability, values/abilities, family/religion, finances/chores, physical attraction/passionate romance, liking/ friendship, and fidelity. Note that intimacy, passion, and commitment (through fidelity) all matter over the long term.

The fact that communication/support proved most important shows that we need to find partners who can not only communicate effectively how they feel, but also who can listen attentively. Listening is an undervalued skill. We are taught to read and write and even, sometimes, speak effectively. But for the most part, we are never given direct instruction in listening. Some people do not know how to listen. Others do not want to. They are so preoccupied with their own thoughts and problems that they tune another person out in next to no time. If you want to make a major improvement in your relationship in a minimum of time, try listening carefully to what your partner says, and – equally important – showing your empathy by putting yourself in his or her place.

The second cluster is understanding and appreciation of the other. Everyone wants to be understood and appreciated, and more people feel underappreciated than overappreciated. Early on in a relationship, one is well able to find a person's strong points but often seems to miss his or her weak points. On the other hand, after knowing someone for a while, one seems to become expert at finding weak points at the expense of strong points. Relationships would be happier if people were more balanced in their approach and tried to be honest with themselves about both their strengths and weaknesses and those of a partner.

The elements in the third cluster – tolerance and acceptance – are, in the long run, indispensable for a relationship to work. The flaws you can overlook or even find appealing in the short run may wear thin in the long run. Tony and Luanne, for example, seem always to be in debt. Although he blames her, and she, him, both are responsible. Tony has a weakness for stereo equipment and indulges frequently, while Luanne has a weakness for expensive jewelry. Although she gets very excited about each new piece, she is soon ready to move on to the next. Their nearly ruinous financial situation would spell the end of many relationships. They stay together, however, perhaps because each accepts the other's weakness in exchange for acceptance of his or her own.

If your partner cannot accept or at least tolerate you the way you are, you still have at least one option open within the realm of what works. You can change to become more like what your partner wants by exercising the flexibility and modifiability of the fourth cluster. This can be a hazardous venture. If you effect a change in yourself, you have to be sure that it is compatible with your basic personality and character. Otherwise, you may come to resent the change and thereby undermine your relationship. Ultimately, it is unlikely such a change will last: People seldom sustain changes that leave them feeling untrue to themselves.

Some partners may be so sure that what they want for the other is the "right thing" that they strongly encourage the other to seek professional help. To take an extreme case, Kurt was thinking of leaving Trudy, and she thought he was crazy. She begged him to see a therapist, which he did, and he thus gained the strength to leave her.

Being in a relationship is a fine balance between giving up and gaining freedom. When you enter into a committed relationship, you normally give up some freedoms in exchange for gaining others. But if you are to keep things working, the limits you try to set on your partner should be reasonable. If they are not, you may be sowing the seeds of the relationship's destruction.

Margo, for example, was extremely demanding of Hal's time. Not only did she want as much of it as possible, but she wanted him to account for almost every minute of it. When Hal would do things she didn't like, she would react forcefully. Eventually, Hal started lying to keep the peace, and then decided to leave altogether. He got sick both of accounting for every minute of his time, and of lying.

The fifth cluster generally deals with matches in both values and abilities, which I have already discussed. The item in this cluster worthy of special mention, though, is pride in a partner's accomplishments. One is likely to compliment one's partner fairly frequently on his or her accomplishments early in a relationship, but less so as the years pass. People like to be complimented on the things they take pride in, and last year's compliments, or last month's, or last week's, need to be reinforced today.

The sixth cluster pertains to family and religious matters – how you handle children, parents, and religion, which is often integral to family life. The seventh cluster pertains to finance and chores; and the eighth, to physical attraction and romance. The ninth cluster is liking and friendship; and the tenth, the weakest, consists of a single item dealing with exclusive fidelity to the other. Although this cluster came out last, its weakness may be simply a function of the fact that only one item measured exclusive fidelity, and this attribute does not tend to relate strongly to other ones.

There is no magic prescription for exclusive sexual fidelity. Although some couples have so-called open relationships, the large majority expect exclusive fidelity. Different things may work for different people, but "open" relationships work a lot less well in practice than in principle, or at least according to some people's principles. Few people can adjust over the long term to a partner's having sexual relations with others. In more cases then not, sexual jealousy eats the relationship alive, and it does not seem to help that the members of the couple are "allowed" to see others.

Our findings suggest a central difficulty in making relationships work.[6] We found that both partners see themselves as being more understanding, appreciative, tolerant, and accepting. Given these feelings, it is going to be hard to achieve a sense of equity in a relationship: Each partner feels as if he or she is contributing more than half to what makes the relationship work. You must thus try better to understand each other's point of view, and why each of you tends to feel that you are contributing more than half. If you cannot do this, and each partner feels undervalued, the relationship may start to erode.

Role playing helps people understand each other: Next time you discuss a serious matter, reverse roles, and do your best to think like your partner. You may come to understand better why he or she feels like the greater contributor, and your partner may start to understand why you feel that way.

Our study also found that issues of family and religion as well as of finances and chores took on more importance as a relationship developed. Thus, pragmatic issues take on greater importance as the couple has to adjust to the realities of being together and getting on in the everyday world.

Our findings indicate that one of the reasons relationships "go bad" is that the things that matter earlier are different from the things that matter later; but we tend to choose partners on the basis of the things that matter earlier rather than later in a relationship. Couples would be wise to discuss early in a relationship pragmatic issues such as having and bringing up a family, religious differences, and handling of finances and chores. These discussions should take place as soon as partners feel there is a good chance that they may wish to stay together on a long-term or permanent basis. It is probably no coincidence that couples entering into second marriages often have a more pragmatic orientation than do couples entering into first marriages: The couples with the experience of a marriage (or more than one) behind them better realize how important pragmatic issues can become.

We also found that participants perceive their relationships as currently more deficient in intimacy than when they first fell in love; thus, as couples start to operate more smoothly, with less disruption, their feelings of intimacy will decrease.

Women tended to view their relationships as being in poorer shape than did men. It has generally been found that women are, at least on the average, more attuned to what is going on in a relationship than are men. They are also more likely to file petitions for divorce.

The Importance of Various Attributes over Time

We found four attributes of relationships to increase in importance over the three durations: sharing values, willingness to change in response to each other, willingness to tolerate each other's flaws, and match in religious beliefs. The second and third items are of particular interest because they show the importance of flexibility in a relationship. To make things work, either you need to change in a way that better suits your partner, or your partner has to come to accept an aspect of your behavior as "the way you are" and as something not likely to change.

Three attributes of relationships decreased in importance over the three segments of time: interestingness to each other, handling of each other's parents, and listening attentively to each other. One can see why handling of parents would become, on the average, less important. Parents often try to have a say in whether a given relationship turns serious. But once it has, in fact, done so, the parental impact decreases.

The decreasing importance of interestingness suggests that partners tend over time to find outside interests. But this decrease, coupled with the decrease in the perceived importance of listening attentively, does not bode well. If partners perceive maintaining the other's interest and listening as less important over time, they may stop working on two of the things that could matter most in the long term. People may be mistaken in assigning decreasing importance to these elements over time, and pay for their mistake in terms of relationships that do, in fact, become less intimate. If you want to maintain intimacy, then listen attentively and try to remain interesting to each other.

Five attributes were found to increase in importance in relationships from short to medium duration, and afterward to decrease in importance: physical attractiveness, ability to make love, ability to empathize, knowledge of what each other is like, and expression of affection toward each other. Just one attribute was found to decrease in importance and then to increase: match in intellectual level.

Why should aspects connected to passion – physical attractiveness, ability to make love, affection – first increase in importance and then decrease? Early on, when a couple is very passionately in love, sheer physical technique and how attractive a person is may be overwhelmed in importance by the thrill of just being in love. As the heat of the love begins to decrease, as it usually does, and a relationship starts to cool, the thrill of being in love may no longer be sufficient to compensate for, say, lack of technique in bed. The "honeymoon" period having ended, partners may experience disillusionment as they see each other through glasses whose rosiness is fading. But these passion-related elements decrease in importance over the very long term, probably in part because of changing expectations about what each person, and an intimate relationship, can reasonably offer an older adult.

There were some interesting sex differences. First, males and females agreed that female physical attractiveness is more important than male physical attractiveness. Second, males believed that shared interests are more important than did females. Third, males believed that the ability to make love is more important than did females. Fourth, males and females agreed that male financial ability is more important than female financial ability. Fifth, females believed that handling of parents is more important than did males; however, both males and females agreed that handling of the female's parents is more important than handling of the male's parents. Sixth, females believed that exclusive fidelity is more important than did males; but males believed that exclusive fidelity is more important for women than for men, whereas women believed that it is equally important for both partners. Seventh, males rated more highly the importance of their willingness to do chores than females rated the importance of male willingness to do chores. Eighth, females believed that ability to get along with the other's friends is more important than did males. Finally, males believed that match in religious beliefs is more important than did females.

These patterns of sex differences show that old sexual stereotypes do not die easily. Even today, the beliefs of men and women are surprisingly sex-stereotypical: Women's looks count more than men's, for example, and it is men who should be judged for their ability to generate income. Perhaps the most troubling result, from some points of view, is the double standard of men, but not women, with respect to sexual fidelity. The results clearly showed that men believe that sexual fidelity *is* important – for women.

Attributes Changing over Time

We found that match in religious beliefs increases over time. But many things decrease over time: ability to communicate with each other, physical attractiveness, having good times, sharing interests, ability to make love, ability to listen, respect for each other, and romantic love for each other.

It would be easy to find these results depressing. Many important aspects of a relationship are viewed as on a continual downswing. Not much is seen as on the upswing: People seem to become less and less happy in their relationships as time passes. Actually, our results are even more discouraging than they look, because these data are for relationships in which people have, in fact, stayed together. The data would almost certainly have been worse had we included ratings of relationships in which couples had broken up.

In statistics, *statistical regression* describes the effect whereby a person who does particularly well at something one time is likely, on the average, not to do as well the next time around; conversely, someone who does unusually poorly on one round is likely to do better the next time around. Statistical regression explains why the baseball player rated as the most valuable rookie during his first year on a team usually does not equal that record of performance in the second year. It also explains why the least valuable player will usually do better in his second year – if he is still allowed to play.

Something of a statistical-regression effect operates in relationships and provides one explanation of why many aspects of relationships seem to get worse over time. When two people meet and decide to form a relationship, the chances are that each is at a point in life when he or she is particularly well suited to the other. Otherwise, they would not stay together. But as people change, statistical regression alone would predict that over time the people are likely to become less suited to each other. For many couples, there is almost nowhere to go except down.

There is not much that can be done about the effect of statistical regression. We can, though, try to keep growing together rather than apart, and this means paying attention to each other, listening, and doing what we can to remain an integral part of each other's life.

We also found that relationships seem to go through at least one hard point, or crisis, and most probably go through more than one. Whether it is called the "seven-year itch" (which may come after fewer or more than seven years) or something else, there appears to be a decline in exclusive fidelity, tolerance, and acceptance of each other after some years, but these things improve later on. This result does not, by any means, guarantee improvement if you and your partner stay together. It is based only on people who have stayed together, and might have been different if we had asked people to rate relationships in which there had been a breakup.

Again, there were interesting sex differences, which overwhelmingly indicated that males perceived the relationship as better than did females. First, males rated communication as better than did females. Males rated their communication skills as higher than the females', whereas females rated their communication skills as higher than the males'. Second, males and females agreed that women are better at finding time to spend with men than the latter are at finding time to spend with women. Third, males rated love making in the relationship as better than did females. Fourth, males rated the financial situation as better than did females. Fifth, males rated handling of parents as better than did females. Sixth, males rated listening as better in the relationship than did females. Seventh, females rated exclusive fidelity as higher in the relationship than did males (indicating that there may be some lack of knowledge on the part of the females). Eighth, males rated tolerance of flaws as higher than did females. Ninth, males rated romantic love as higher than did females. Finally, males rated liking as higher than did females.

Of the many possible reasons men may be more positive about their relationships than are women, any or all may be correct. One possibility is that women are more astute, and that men are denying the problems in their relationships. A second possibility is that the women are more critical and expect more of a relationship. But most likely, both the men and the women are right. The relationship actually works differentially well for the two of them, with better outcomes, on the average, for men than for women. Mortality statistics actually bear out this argument: Single men die earlier and are more susceptible to sickness and accidents than are married men; but the reverse is true for women. Thus, even in concrete, health-related terms, men stand more to gain from long-term relationships than do women, even though it seems that they are often the more reluctant sex to enter into them.

Prediction of Success

We predicted ratings of satisfaction with the relationship from the variables in our study. Two attributes showed an increasing pattern of correlation with success: finding time to be with each other and willingness to change in response to each other. In other words, higher scores on these attributes became more predictive over time of satisfaction with the relationship. People who were satisfied with their relationships found more time to be with each other and were willing to change for each other. Finding time may actually be a proxy for other things. In particular, you are more likely to find time to be with someone if you positively enjoy being with the person, and you are less likely to find the time if you find every minute of his or her company aversive. Thus, it may not be the time itself that matters so much as what spending that time represents.

Perhaps the most important result to come out of this set of analyses is the difference in what predicts happiness in a relationship for men versus women. Men weigh more the abstraction of the way things *should be,* whereas women weigh more the concrete situation as it actually exists.

In summary, what matters to a relationship seems to change substantially over time, both with respect to what is important to it and with respect to what actually characterizes it. We might better predict long-term satisfaction with relationships if we gave more attention to the variables that will matter in the long run, and perhaps a bit less attention to those that matter in the short run.

PART V

When Cupid's Arrow Falls: Love in Our Lifetime: Endings

12
Decay of Relationships

The evidence generally suggests that marital happiness tends to decline over time.[1] It has been suggested that the decline in marital satisfaction is due to two primary factors: fading of the passionate romance that characterizes premarital courtship, and the almost inevitable decrease in intimacy and compatibility.[2] When passion and intimacy fade, loss of commitment soon follows. Presumably, when people marry, they often feel that they are "best fits" to each other. If this is indeed true, or close to true, then, as noted in the previous chapter, almost any changes that occur are likely to be for the worse. In an interesting twist on this "best fit" notion, it has been suggested that people often get involved in relationships because of their own self-doubts, particularly doubts about their personal worth.[3] Once in a successful relationship, one's self-image improves because of the reinforcement provided by the partner. But then the relationship may decline because the need that motivated the relationship has been fulfilled.

For example, Carl, who was very insecure, looked long and hard for a woman who could bolster his fragile ego, and finally found such a one in Marybeth. She was exceptional: Most women tired of constantly bolstering a man who was so pathetically insecure, but Marybeth seemed to have boundless energy in this regard. Finally, she gave so much that Carl actually began to feel better about himself. But, by now, he had come to associate his relationship with Marybeth with his feelings of insecurity, and no longer wanted to deal with those feelings or even acknowledge that they had ever existed. So he went out and found himself a new love. He also found out, when Marybeth left him, that his feelings of insecurity had never really ended. He returned to Marybeth, who took him back, and they are again in the only type of relationship that seems to work for them, with Marybeth continually feeding Carl's weak ego.

The decline in happiness may not be limited to marriages. It is known, for example, that couples who live together before marriage have a higher rate of divorce than do those who do not live together in advance.[4] One reason, noted earlier, may be that the kinds of people who live together before marriage are just more likely to divorce later on. But another reason may be that people who live together before marriage tend to have been together longer than people who did not at the time of marriage. According to this view, prior cohabitors are more likely to divorce simply because when they marry their relationship is already farther along on the route toward decay and dissolution.[5]

The course of happiness in marriage does not always lead downhill. Some investigators believe that marital satisfaction is at a high during the early years, goes down during the middle years, and goes up again during the later years.[6] One reason for this U-shaped pattern is probably the effect of raising children. It is well documented that the coming of children into a marriage creates new strains and is associated with a decrease in marital happiness. As the children grow up and eventually move away, marriages again improve.[7]

Children are not the only source of increasing discontent in close relationships. Another is what might be referred to as *role strain* – the conflict over who is supposed to do what in a relationship.[8] While at one time role expectations for men and women were relatively clear, today they are not. With all the pressures on couples to earn income, have children, maintain a nice house, entertain themselves, and have a meaningful relationship, many couples find that the magnitude of the tasks confronting them exceeds their ability to get them done. And their ability to get their tasks done may be further hindered by confusion over what tasks are whose responsibility. Over time, the strain of such role confusion can become a major source of discontent.

People are often most likely to question the motives of others when things are not going well.[9] For example, Ann's husband, Bill, worked late, but she never questioned it while her relationship with him was going well. But then things started going less well, and she started to ask questions and make attributions about behavior that in the past she had always taken for granted. And she started with Bill's working late at the office. Whereas earlier she hadn't given it a second – or at least a third – thought, now she found herself wondering what he was doing and with whom. She didn't know for a fact that he was doing anything with anyone, but once she got started thinking that way, she found it difficult to shut it off. As it happens, Bill was working late because he was working late, and when the couple resolved their difficulties, the doubts went away that were, for Ann, symptomatic of their difficulties.

We also understand the reasons for our own behavior and that these reasons justify that behavior.[10] During conflict, we start seeing things differently. We may become less objective and impartial and more egocentric and self-serving. We believe that we know why we act the way we do and that our motives are good. The other, however, may act from rather dubious motives.

Such conflicts regarding motives are often unresolvable.[11] Initially, most conflicts will concern who did what, but eventually such conflicts will turn to the further issue of why. Thus, the two partners, each believing that he or she is motivated by good reasons and intentions, may reach an impasse in which each protests his or her own innocence and points out the other's guilt. Once arguments concentrate on innocence and guilt, the partners become increasingly self-serving rather than trying to resolve the conflict.

For example, Jimmy and Lea, like many couples, seem almost never to resolve any of their arguments. They start off arguing over matters of substance but quickly come to matters of guilt and innocence. For example, if they argue over money, an argument over what should be purchased degenerates into an argument over who is a spendthrift. Once the argument has taken this turn, there is no longer any hope of resolution, because matters of guilt and innocence are not ones they are in a position to resolve; and the issues they are in a position to resolve never really get discussed.

Once conflict arises, the partners to it become especially susceptible to an error in thinking discussed earlier, the *fundamental attribution error* – the tendency to see the causes of their own behavior as *situational* (controlled by events in the environment) but the causes of the behavior of others as *dispositional* (controlled by what they are like as people).[12] In other words, when one does things that might seem unpleasant to others or even to oneself, one is likely to cite the situation as the cause of one's actions: One has been pressured into it by others, or there seemed to be no other choice, or the situation dictated a quick decision. In contrast, one tends to view other people as motivated by their own dispositions. Thus, if someone does something you don't like, you tend to interpret it as confirming your suspicions about who he or she really is.

Clearly, these conflicts about motives are destructive, because one tends to see oneself as good and the other as not so good. Indeed, much research now confirms Kelley's view that the results of attributional conflicts tend to be negative and destructive.[13] If one does indeed conclude that one is stuck with somebody who isn't a very good person, one may consider terminating the relationship or finding another one. Research suggests that women are somewhat more susceptible to a negative attributional style than are men: In other words, women are more likely to be critical, of themselves as well as of others (although the evidence in support of this finding is not crystal clear).[14] Perhaps this is one reason for the finding that women tend to be less happy with their relationships than men are.[15]

One study investigated how happy and unhappy couples make attributions.[16] The participants were asked to imagine that their spouses had behaved in a certain way, to rate the possible causes for the behavior, and to indicate what they would feel and do in response to the behavior. Half of the imagined situations involved favorable actions; and the other half, unfavorable actions by the spouse. Partners in happy marriages generally saw favorable actions by the spouse as likely to occur, as resulting from the spouse's wishes as well as their own, and as drawing out favorable reactions from themselves. Unfavorable actions, in contrast, were viewed as relatively rare and involuntary. Thus, the unfavorable actions received a situational rather than a dispositional attribution, even though they pertained to the other partner. Unhappy couples showed opposite results: Unfavorable behavior was seen as common, extensive, deliberate, and provoking. Moreover, favorable behavior was generally discounted. Supporting these results, it has been found that happy couples tend to emphasize the role of dispositional causes for favorable behavior, and the role of situational factors for unfavorable behavior. Unhappy couples tend to do the reverse.[17]

What all this means is that it may not be people's actions but how we perceive those actions that affects, and is affected by, the quality of a relationship. The very same actions may be perceived in radically different ways, depending on whether a person is happy or unhappy with the state of his or her relationship. Thus it was with Ann, who did not make a negative attribution about her husband's working late until she became unhappy with the relationship.

Arthur and Grace provide another case in point. For a long time they had a reasonably happy, if somewhat dull, relationship. Then Arthur met someone else and entered into an affair with her. But he could neither accept responsibility for the affair nor admit that, to the extent his relationship with Grace was unexciting, it was at least half his fault. Arthur became extremely critical of Grace, lambasting her for behavior that she had shown all along but that he had never before criticized or even felt particularly critical of. He was using the new negative attributions to excuse his infidelity.

In sum, if we are happy in a relationship, we tend to magnify the importance of the positive and to minimize the importance of the negative, whereas if we are unhappy in a relationship, we do the opposite.[18] This tendency is important, because negative emotions and behavior are more predictive of satisfaction than are positive emotions and behaviors, which is to say that the negative are better relationship killers than the positive ones are relationship savers.[19] Indeed, research suggests that satisfied couples have a ratio of at least five positive interactions for every one negative one.[20] If one partner attempts to discuss the negative interactions, and the other refuses or denies their existence, the prognosis for the relationship is especially poor.[21]

Of course, what is perceived as a negative interaction can depend on how happy we are in the first place. Dissatisfied partners tend to view the same interaction more negatively than do satisfied partners.[22] Moreover, dissatisfied partners are less accurate decoders of their partner's intentions in communication than are satisfied partners, meaning that once a negative spiral begins, it can be very hard to stop it because of inaccurate interpretations of the partner's intentions.[23]

If we are unhappy, we tend to emphasize situational factors for the positive and dispositional factors for the negative.[24] For example, when you are unhappy with someone, you may attribute that person's being nice to the weather, but see bad behavior as intrinsic to him or her. Or when someone you don't trust is nice to you, you may interpret the niceness as ingratiation – as an attempt to get something.

Unhappy couples are more responsive than happy couples to negative events, such as disagreements. Among the happy couples, the number of negative events occurring during a day has only a weak relationship to overall daily satisfaction; whereas for unhappy couples, the number of negative events is highly related to daily satisfaction.[25] But unhappy couples also appeared to be more responsive to positive events, such as news of a bonus or of a child's success in school – a finding that suggests that unhappy couples are more reactive over all. In other words, each member responds more strongly to things. This finding suggests that the partners in an unhappy relationship who make a deliberate effort to behave positively toward each other are likely to notice and respond in kind. As the positive actions increase, the unhappy couple may become happier. This outcome will not occur, however, unless the couple can learn not to attribute positive actions to particular situations. In other words, if one makes excuses for a positive action rather than just enjoying it, it will not have a positive effect. For example, each member of the couple might say that the other member is behaving in a more positive way because of an agreement to improve the relationship rather than because he or she is genuinely a good person. Getting out of this morass is no easy feat.

There is yet another step one can take toward improving one's relationships.[26] One can assume more responsibility for what happens in a relationship. If you credit yourself for the good things that happen but blame the other person for the bad things, there is no hope for improvement. But if you can make a concerted and good-faith effort to see the other person's point of view, and put yourself in his or her shoes, you may see how you also are responsible for the problems in the relationship. Instead of assigning all or almost all of the blame to the other person, you should take on some of it yourself and try to understand how the other person's actions may, in part, be reactions to your actions. Having a sense of control in marital interaction is crucial for happiness: Each member of the couple needs to feel some sense of responsibility for what has happened, and some sense of control for what can happen in the future.[27] Indeed, if you feel that your actions are totally determined by the situation, you have little control over yourself, and if you feel that the other person's actions are totally due to the way he or she is, you have no control over him or her. Thus, you need to acknowledge your role as a source of your own behavior and the role of the situational origins of the other's behavior, thereby overcoming the fundamental attribution error.

This is not to say that we should always follow a path looking for improvement. Some relationships genuinely do not and cannot work, or simply were not meant to be. With a partner who is physically or mentally abusive and unable to change, the search for good reasons for his or her behavior may not lead to a more favorable outcome. Perhaps the hardest part of a relationship is knowing when to try to salvage things and when not to. Sometimes people need the help of an objective third party, such as a therapist, in order to sort things out.

In interpersonal interactions, people often do not hear each other. One or the other partner may say the same thing time after time, and be amazed, if not insulted, that he or she does not seem to be understood correctly. The listener is hearing from his or her own vantage point and set of categories. As a result, the conflict never gets settled.

Loss of intimacy through poor communication is a major predictor of relationship decay. One study, for example, found that spouses' ratings of the positive versus negative nature of each other's communications was a strong predictor of satisfaction or dissatisfaction up to five years after the ratings were given.[28] Sometimes one is simply unable to understand either the other individual's behavior or the thoughts or feelings that generate it. For one reason or another, the other person's way of seeing things is just too different from one's own. When such lack of understanding occurs, the optimal solution is probably not to fall back on one's own way of looking at things. Sometimes, one has to make the leap of faith, trusting that the other person has good intentions. Obviously, one cannot have faith in everyone. But actions and motives that are not understood at one point in life can often be understood later. If you really want reconciliation and to keep the relationship, it is wise to give yourself a fair stretch of time to understand the other person, and avoid letting conflict escalate into successively higher levels.

People create scenarios to make sense of conflicts and, more generally, what is going on not only during a relationship but after it ends. Often neither party to a relationship quite understands what went wrong. It is as though the relationship, in its final days, took on a life of its own – perhaps a life that seemed almost incomprehensible to either partner. Breakups are usually distressing, and in order to deal satisfactorily with that distress, one may create hypothetical scripts about what went wrong. One may attribute the breakup to the other person's disloyalty, inconsideration, or greed; or, in part, to one's own lack of effort in trying to make things work. But more often than not, the script points to the other person as bearing a major share of the responsibility for the breakup. People may need such self-serving scenarios to get over a relationship and move on.

If one wants to get over a relationship and put it out of mind, one needs to give it some completion, and a scenario accounting for what went wrong may fulfill this need. Often the creation of such scripts is a difficult task, because they almost never do full justice to what happened; and, at some level, one knows that the script one has created is an oversimplification. The scenario may nevertheless help one to move on.

Scenarios of this kind almost always are inaccurate to some degree, and their benefit may ultimately be offset by their inaccuracies. For one thing, they prevent you from relating in a meaningful way to the partner in the former relationship. You may continue to have to work with the partner, either in your job or in bringing up the children. Better understanding of the partner and of his or her relation to yourself helps you to work with your former partner.

Breaking up can also help you better to understand yourself and the way you relate to others. The more inaccurate your understanding of the relationship, the less understanding of yourself and others you achieve; indeed, you may learn little from the breakup and proceed to repeat the same mistakes in future relationships. If you hope to learn from your past and to apply what you have learned to new relationships, then you need at least a fairly accurate understanding of what went wrong and of how to avoid it in future relationships.

Finally, to the extent that your understanding is inaccurate and you know it, you may continue to obsess over the relationships. You would do better to try to improve the accuracy of the account of the relationship so as to conclude the story of the past relationship. If you cannot do so, the relationship may live on in your head, always looking for a resolution that you know you have not yet found. You will be unable to move on the way you would like to a new relationship, as considered in Chapter 13.

13

Dissolution of and New Beginnings for Relationships

Many relationships ultimately cease to work, and it is helpful to know not only *why* they have ceased – for example, loss of intimacy, passion, or commitment – but also *how*. Diane Vaughan, a sociologist, addresses the question of what happens when relationships stop working.[1]

IT STARTS WITH A SECRET

According to Vaughan, disengagement, or what she calls "uncoupling," begins with a secret. One of the partners in the relationship begins to feel uncomfortable in it. This discomfort may begin early, even before the wedding, or after many years. But the critical thing is that the disengagement begins unilaterally and quietly: The dissatisfied partner generally says nothing. He or she may not even consciously realize that something is wrong, or just what is wrong; or be certain of the implications of the feelings: Will they lead to a separation or are they just temporary and of passing importance? Since the dissatisfied partner does not want to say anything before being absolutely sure of what is wrong, he or she creates a private world in which to mull over those feelings. It would be better for all if the partner communicated the dissatisfaction, but, often, the communication does not take place. Vaughan's theory is basically about how loss of intimacy leads to withdrawal of commitment, slowly and step by step.

In creating this private world, the dissatisfied partner, generally unintentionally, initiates a breach of communication. The partner, while not necessarily viewing himself or herself as lying, nevertheless withholds information that would be important to the other partner. Secrecy permits one to think about things, to develop plans, and generally to figure out what to do. But the other partner, being uninformed of the dissatisfaction, is powerless to do anything about the situation. Eventually the dissatisfied partner – the initiator – begins to try to convey his or her dissatisfaction to the partner but finds it difficult, because he or she may still not have quite figured out the problem. Unable to communicate fully and accurately the source of the dissatisfaction, the initiator will generally not directly confront the partner in a way that allows the latter to address the basic issues, but rather displays dissatisfaction in subtle ways, many of which may not even be understood by the partner as indicating global dissatisfaction.

Vaughan points out that the initiator's first attempts to communicate unhappiness are, in part, an attempt to save the relationship. By indicating dissatisfaction, the initiator is trying to change the partner or the relationship so as to create a situation acceptable to the partner. The efforts of the initiator seldom result in quick success. This lack of success is hardly surprising, as the partner does not yet realize the nature and extent of the dissatisfaction. Indeed, some of the initiator's remarks may camouflage rather than reveal the sources of dissatisfaction. So the initiator remains unhappy, and the partner is likely not to be in a position to do anything about it.

The initiator, unhappy with the relationship, turns to alternative sources of satisfaction – outside activities, new friends, or an affair. As the initiator begins to form a new life, the partner may wonder what is going on and why. The partner may attribute the changes to second childhood or a further sowing of oats, while the relationship itself is the true source of dissatisfaction. Eventually the initiator will create a separate social life, which may take increasing amounts of time and energy. The partner may be shut out of this new life and not even know the full extent of what is happening in it.

Often the initiator will enter into a new meaningful relationship, sexual or not, as a means for venting dissatisfaction and frustration and for finding an alternative. The new relationship, which may even be partially based on fantasy, may satisfy the need of the initiator to form new ties. This situation further increases the need for secrecy, so that the gulf between the initiator and the partner is likely to expand.

What happens in disengagement is in many respects the exact opposite of what happens when one is drawn to someone else initially. In falling in love with someone, one tends to concentrate on his or her favorable traits. One notices how one is similar to and compatible with this new partner, and attempts to view any differences as complementary. As a relationship grows, there occurs the "fallen angel" phenomenon: No other can live up to the degree of perfection one may have hoped for. But if the relationship starts to disengage, the focus of the initiator shifts to the unfavorable qualities of the partner, who is then redefined in terms of his or her objectionable traits. The initiator concentrates on the points of difference with the partner, seeing them now as disturbing and unattractive. The initiator is likely to recast the history of the relationship, seeing negative aspects in what before had been positively construed events. The relationship is suddenly seen in a new and unfavorable light. The initiator becomes prey to the fact that there is no objective historical account of the past, and shapes the past to fit the needs of the present.

The initiator's increasing dissatisfaction becomes more apparent both to others and to the initiator. Whereas earlier the initiator may have expressed discontent with the hope of saving the relationship, now his or her intent is to convince the partner that the relationship is troubled or perhaps even cannot be salvaged. The initiator expresses dissatisfaction not only to the partner but to others as well. The initiator informs close friends and colleagues that all is not as it should be in his or her personal relationship with the partner. There may be jokes about the partner, angry exclamations, or subtle digs. But the message is conveyed in one way or another. The initiator is likely to avoid those with a vested interest in continuing the relationship, because they make the initiator uncomfortable. Instead, the initiator is likely to select as friends at this time only those who will provide support for his or her intended moves.

By this time, it is extremely common that the initiator has found a *transitional person:* that is, someone who helps the initiator through the transition that is beginning to play a greater part in the initiator's life. The transitional person, who may be a lover or a friend, is someone who helps the initiator ease himself or herself out of the old relationship. Sometimes there may be more than one transitional person, each person taking on a different role. For example, a psychotherapist and a lover would play different roles, each helping the initiator to leave an old life and find a new one.

As the initiator more and more expresses increasing discontent, the social perception of the couple may change. The relationship is likely to be viewed as in distress. Sometimes the partner may be the last to know just how amiss things have become. Initiators are likely to look for information about the transition they are experiencing, either through books, magazines, plays, movies, or whatever. Noticing how others have dealt with similar transitions, they try to apply this information to their own lives. The initiator pushes toward a new life and is gradually pulled away from the old one. The initiator may become increasingly detached from the old relationship and spend ever less time engaging in it. As initiator and partner grow further apart, the role of separate friends is likely to become greater. Whereas, before, the emphasis in the relationship may have been upon mutual friends and acquaintances, now each individual looks for his or her own support group.

Symbolic behavior may become especially important at this time, such as the initiator's removal of the wedding ring (to which he or she has suddenly become "allergic") or the undermining of actions that had been done together but are now suddenly done apart, such as going on trips. By now, the initiator is well out of the relationship, whereas the partner may still be firmly entrenched within it. For the partner, the relationship is still central to his or her life and identity, and he or she may now seriously wonder about what is going on.

It often seems incredible that two people can live together and one go so far afield without the other's noticing. Partners often describe themselves as unaware or only vaguely aware of things having gone wrong. At the same time, the initiator is likely to report that he or she has made repeated efforts to apprise the partner of the seriousness of the situation. Clearly, a major breakdown in communication has taken place, because the two partners see the situation as so very different.

What has happened, according to Vaughan, is that the partners have colluded in a cover-up. The initiator is indirect and subtle in order to protect one or both partners. The partner takes what is said more or less at face value, not looking to find any deeper meaning. If the initiator makes one complaint after another, these complaints are taken as stated rather than as symptomatic of a deeper problem in the relationship. While recognizing that something is wrong, the partner may view it as a normal part of ongoing relationships. The partner may keep things private, as the commonplace view in our society is that marital problems should be a private matter. At the same time, the initiator, viewing the relationship as deeply troubled, is likely communicating his or her dissatisfaction publicly. The partner may believe that any problem is not in the relationship but in the initiator and suggest that the initiator seek professional or other help. Ironically, in so doing, the initiator finds a new ally in the march toward disengagement. Since it is the nature of therapy that the patient stresses his or her point of view, the chances are good that the situation will be defined in terms satisfactory to the initiator rather than to the partner.

Eventually, the collusion breaks down, and the cover-up fails. Now confrontations are likely to become direct. The initiator who is far enough along, and certain that he or she wants out, is likely to become bolder, having less to risk by direct expression of his or her feelings. For the initiator, the question now may be not whether to leave, but how. At this point, the initiator may start making concrete preparations for a new life, such as a secret bank account or the hiding of assets from the partner. The initiator may talk to a lawyer and start devising a plan for how to get out. He or she may even have a date in mind at which time the decision to split is to be communicated to the partner. As the date begins to loom, the initiator continues preparing for a new life. Often the date does not quite materialize when it is supposed to. Something else may come up – such as a crisis in the extended family or problems on the job or of health – and temporarily delay the planned date of separation.

By now, the partner is likely to view the relationship as troubled, whereas the initiator is likely to view it as over. The confrontation emerges, but the initiator is unwilling to take responsibility for it. Rather, he or she tries to find some way of shifting at least some of the burden of the conflict to the partner. Sometimes the initiator tries to goad the partner further into making a "fatal mistake," which is likely to be a manifestation of some behavior that the initiator can describe as totally unacceptable. This mistake may also be a failure to initiate a behavior that the initiator would view as necessary. For example, if the partner reacts with a highly emotional outburst, the initiator may say that this proves what he or she has feared all along – that the partner is wholly irrational. The initiator is likely to decrease interaction with the partner and may even start violating formerly tacit rules of the relationship. The partner, eventually realizing that something is seriously wrong, may take on the role of a detective, trying to figure out just what is going on. He or she may look for evidence in the initiator's actions, personal possessions, or through communications from others.

Once an overt confrontation has been reached, both partners are ready and willing to acknowledge that the relationship is deeply troubled, and are likely to enter into negotiations to salvage it. But the two members are not negotiating on equal footing, because the initiator feels that he or she has already tried. Attempts at communication and to improve the relationship have been made, and nothing seems to work. For the initiator, then, the relationship may already be over or past the point of no return. Thus, although the partner makes a belated but hopeful attempt to render change, the initiator may merely appear to try while intending to ease his or her way out of the relationship. The partner is likely to devote increased priority and energy to the relationship and to make a concerted effort to persuade the initiator to stay. This effort may save the relationship, but usually it fails because by this time the initiator is well on the way toward a radically different life. The initiator has become, in some sense, a different person, and may feel as if the partner does not know him or her any more. Any changes are likely to be superficial and not touching the root of the real problem in the relationship. Moreover, both partners are likely to sense that this is a period of trying, and that what is happening is not really the relationship but something else – an attempt to find the relationship. Although the partner seeks stability in returning to what was, the relationship seems to keep reverting to its degenerated state.

At this point, the power balance in the relationship is fundamentally unequal. The initiator, as the less involved person, has far greater power than the partner, because it is the former who has the power to continue the relationship or to leave it. Ultimately, the initiator may suggest a temporary separation, which makes the state of the relationship a matter of public note. The separation is likely to lead the couple even further apart: Whereas the partner may see the separation as the last hope for reconciliation, the initiator is likely to see it as the first physical step toward the ultimate termination of the relationship.

It is sometimes asked, who finds the separation easier – the man or the woman? Often it is said that the man finds it easier, if only for economic reasons. But, according to Vaughan, much more important than the sex of the individual is the role in the separation: The initiator is far better prepared for the separation and is likely to be the one who finds it easier. The initiator has been gradually easing into the separated role; whereas, for the partner, the separation may be sudden, with little preparation or forethought. This is not to say that the separation may not be hard for the initiator. Moreover, the partner may, in some instances, try to make life harder for the initiator out of spite or revenge. The partner may hope to prove to the initiator that life on his or her own is substantially worse than life as a couple. But the partner's attempts to make life difficult for the initiator are likely to boomerang, making the initiator only more determined to stay outside the relationship.

The total amount of mourning and grief suffered by each member of the former couple may be equal, but for the initiator it has been spread out over a longer time. The other partner, who must mourn in a relatively shorter time, may be at wit's end. Each must find new friends and try to maintain some of the old friendships from the marriage. A competition may ensue whereby each of the partners tries to sway friends of the now separated couple toward his or her point of view. Usually it is difficult for people to be friends with both partners, and they may be forced to make a choice. Some may withdraw entirely, unwilling to choose between the two members of the couple who have now been torn apart.

What started off as a temporary separation is likely to become permanent, because much of what happens during the separation involves increasing independence of the partners from each other. Moreover, one partner may so antagonize the other that whatever little hope there may once have been is now lost. Now the second partner must go through the same redefinition of the relationship that the initiator underwent earlier. The partner, like the initiator of the past, must begin to see the chinks in the armor and define the now dying relationship as one that perhaps was not so good after all. The partner may not wish to redefine the relationship negatively; but, according to Vaughan, such a redefinition is important for the partner's well-being because of the need to put the relationship behind one. The redefinition may be hard, especially if the partner has latent feelings of failure. In order successfully to undergo the transition, the partner must realize that both members of the former couple are partially responsible.

What happens now may seem strange in many respects to both partners, because they have now become outside observers of each other's life. Much of what they hear about the other they may hear from third persons, whether friends or children. They must now both come to view the relationship as beyond saving, although many partners do not take this view until the initiator has formed a new public relationship with somebody else.

Reconciliation can occur, and occasionally does, but Vaughan points out that it is difficult. To achieve a genuine reconciliation, both of the partners must redefine the other person and their relationship in a positive way. Moreover, they have to change the public definition of themselves – now that of a separated couple. The reconciliation cannot be a return to what was, but rather must be a transition to yet something else. If it is a return, it is much more likely to fail than to succeed. It will work only if a new relationship is formed that is stronger, more durable, and more realistic than the one the partners had before.

This process of disengagement, as characterized by Vaughan, does not describe all breakups equally well. Many breakups do, however, show similar patterns; and, as a sociologist, Vaughan has documented them with striking success.

CREATING A SCRIPT OF DISENGAGEMENT

Another classic work on disengagement is by Robert Weiss.[2] Weiss opens by considering why the rate of marital separation has risen over the years. Of several reasons, the first is socioeconomic: Both men and women are better off economically than they once were, and modern society places great emphasis on individual rights, so both partners are better able to be socially and economically independent. Second, whereas divorce was once considered scandalous, it no longer is; thus, people, deterred in the past by the social stigma of divorce, are more likely to pursue this course now. Third, organized religion has become more permissive, with even some Roman Catholic priests increasingly accepting the notion of secular divorce. Some of us value what we see as our rise to the unimpeded pursuit of happiness; and if this route requires a divorce, so be it.

Weiss believes that during the separation, each partner forms an account or a history of the marital failure, which is essentially a script describing the relationship and its downfall. Each sees the shrinking of a triangle of love from a different point of view. The account may include a few or many of the major events that signified what went wrong. It is not only a chronology but an assignment of blame: Through the account, the partners partition the blame between themselves, also including the effect of outside persons and circumstances on the separation. Thus, they account for both dispositions and situations in their account.

The accounts of husband and wife are likely to differ, and an outside listener hearing the two might not even realize that they are accounts of the same marriage. Each partner has selected and reinterpreted events in such a way as to render them favorable to the self and palatable in providing an understanding of what now seems to have gone wrong. In many of these accounts, Weiss found that men or women mourned not the marriage but rather the years they devoted to it. Another common theme was that each spouse wanted different things from life. Some accounts stressed chronic failings of the other spouse; and others noted things that, although irritating, would scarcely seem as important to an outside observer as they did to the separated couple. Some partners had lost their ability to talk to each other, and others engaged in infidelity. Although infidelity may contribute to the demise of a marriage, it is itself often a symptom of things that have already gone wrong. A common aspect of the failing marriage is the existence of interchanges that have the effect of invalidating each partner's view of himself or herself. Even though they may not mean to, members of the couple may look for their own self-validation at the expense of the other. Rejection may come in many forms, and the members of the couple may have great difficulty in maintaining their self-esteem.

An especially important insight of Weiss lies in his discussion of the erosion of love and the persistence of attachment. Weiss observes that even though the partners' love for each other may well be dissipated, their sense of attachment to each other may remain. Even if they have argued a lot, they miss the arguing. The members of the couple may experience the same kind of separation anxiety that each as a child once experienced when temporarily separated from the mother.

It is important to distinguish between love and attachment. According to Weiss, love usually involves some degree of idealization, trust, identification, and complementarity. Attachment, which usually accompanies love, is a bonding to another that gives rise to feelings of being at home and at ease with the other. Although love and attachment are separate things, it is easy to confuse the two, and some couples inevitably do. On Weiss's view, then, a theory of attachment does not provide a basis for a theory of love.

The loss of attachment can give rise to a wide variety of emotions, including ones as diverse as stress and euphoria. Separation distress is the focusing of attention on the lost person, together with intense discomfort because of the loss. It results not just from being alone but from being without the other person specifically. In separation distress, one may experience apprehension, anxiety, or fear. Some people experience euphoria rather than distress – as though a black cloud has lifted from their lives, or as though they were walking on air. Although this reaction of euphoria seems distinct from distress, Weiss points out that the two may be related: Euphoria may result from the realization that the attachment figure, previously thought to be necessary to your life, really is not, and that you can manage on your own. But such euphoria is just another way of managing the same thing – namely, the loss of the individual to whom you are attached.

Weiss notes several factors that affect separation distress. One is forewarning. Separations that occur after a seemingly good marriage are much more difficult than separations that occur after a seemingly inharmonious marriage. To the partner who has viewed the marriage as satisfactory, the separation may appear to have come from nowhere.

A second factor that affects distress is the length of the marriage. There is a cutoff period of two years, before which the separation distress is considerably less than afterward. Couples in their first two years have not fully integrated their marriage into the fabric of their lives; but after that time, according to Weiss, the length of the marriage seems to make little difference in the amount of distress the members of the couple feel.

A third factor is who is the leaver and who is the left, with the difference between the two apparently involving more the character of the distress than its intensity. However, the definition of which spouse has decided to separate is largely arbitrary, the marriage having become nearly intolerable for both. Only rarely does one spouse decide on the separation while the other opposes it. In contrast, Vaughan argues that, on the average, the person who is left feels the greater distress.

Perhaps Vaughan is closer to the truth. Leaving is tough, but being left is tougher. For one thing, the person who leaves is more likely to be prepared for the split than is the person who is left, who may, in fact, be caught totally off guard. For another thing, it is the leaver who makes the decision, and the person who is left will often not accede willingly to it.

Finally, the leaver is the one exerting the power in the relationship; as a result, the partner may feel not only alone but powerless and perhaps unworthy.

A fourth factor affecting stress is the presence of someone new, who can help deflect some of the sorrow and pain of the separation. While obviously this person cannot take away all of the distress, he or she can help the uncoupled partner to channel energy into building something new and turn it away from reminiscing about something old. Finally, Weiss notes that the quality of the postmarital relationship affects the degree of distress. How the husband and wife treat each other after the separation will be a major determinant of how they adjust. Obviously, better treatment will lead to better adjustment.

Weiss argues that a major consequence of the separation is a disruption of identity. People become unsure of just who they are. To some extent, their social identity, and perhaps their psychological identity as well, is in a state of transition. They may find themselves susceptible to self-deprecation and guilt, whether they are the leaver or the left. They may have problems in planning for the future because of uncertainty of what the future holds. They may find themselves obsessively reviewing the marriage, trying to figure out what went wrong. Ironically, this crisis of identity comes at a time when many decisions have to be made but the ability to make them is impaired. Even ability to work is impaired, and Weiss has found that people in the middle of a separation often do their best at work whose intellectual challenge is engaging but not maximal.

One of the most difficult aspects of the separation is that what was once a well-defined relationship becomes ill defined. Whereas before there may have been certain rules, many of them tacit, now it is not clear what the rules are, and the former partners must redefine their relationship. In some cases, they may have little to do with each other. But more often, their lives are sufficiently entangled so that they need to engage in fairly regular communication, especially if there are children, and they need to make a great effort to figure out what form their relationship will now take. There are likely to be sources of conflicts of interest regarding property division, support, custody of children, visitation rights, and so on – all of which make hammering out a new relationship exceedingly difficult. In many cases, the relationship will become worse than it was before.

Some partners are so averse to separation that they consider reconciliation. It is not known what proportion of separated couples eventually reconcile; but it is known that the further along the couple is toward divorce, the less likely a reconciliation is to take place. If the separation was impulsive, reconciliation may take place quickly. But if it was deliberate, and there is actually a filing for a divorce, the chances are only about one in eight that a reconciliation will eventually take place. It appears that the chance of a reconciliation working out are only about fifty–fifty; and as noted earlier, a redefinition of the relationship is needed in order for the reconciliation to succeed. One danger of reconciliation is that if it does not work, one or both of the members of the couple may have exhausted their resources in terms of being able to initiate or cope with a second separation.

Ultimately, if the separation continues, both members of the now defunct couple need to start over. For both members of the couple, there will be a transition period unlike anything that has come before and probably anything that will happen again: It marks the ending of one period of life and the beginning of the next. A new partner can be more effective than any system for relieving loneliness. But unless one takes the time honestly and realistically to assess what went wrong and what one's contribution was, the same problems may arise in the new relationship that plagued the old. If the separated partners can grow from the experience and correct their weaknesses, the disengagement may ultimately be a cause of bounty in life rather than of despair.

GETTING OVER A RELATIONSHIP

People are often surprised by how difficult – or how easy – it is to get over a relationship.[3] Whether it is easy or hard to get over the other person can depend on a variety of factors, one of which is the difference between one's emotional involvement with the other person and the amount of benefit one actually got from the relationship. People who are highly emotionally involved in a relationship, but actually receive little from it in terms of objective gains and benefits, may find it easier to get over the relationship than they expect. Similarly, people who are not deeply involved emotionally, but benefit a great deal from the relationship, may find it harder than they expect to get over it.[4] Thus, the actual difficulty of getting over a relationship does not necessarily bear out anticipated difficulty.

In helping yourself get over a relationship with another, probably the most important thing is to build your self-esteem and sense of independence. Often when a relationship ends, you cannot imagine living without the other person. Life seems as if it cannot go on. But it will. Or perhaps living without the other person would be possible if you could only find another to take his or her place. People often spend long periods of time looking for another person to help them get out of a particular relationship. In effect, they want to leave one person for another in order to ease the transition. In fact, having another person available may make things easier in the short run, but is not likely to do so in the long run. For one thing, the new relationship is more likely than not ultimately to fail: Because it has been built on a particular set of circumstances, when the situation changes, so will the relationship.

Moreover, residual feelings of guilt in one or the other person may render it difficult to continue the relationship. Finally, there is always the possibility that the person who has left the first individual for the other may leave the other for someone else, or vice versa. Thus, whereas one wants to find supportive friends, one might do better not to have a transition figure who later will not fit into one's life.

For example, Paul and Margie started an office affair that grew into a full-blown romance. Paul was married; Margie was not and never had been. After much soul searching, Paul left his marriage for her. But as soon as he left, a relationship that had been almost conflict free became incredibly conflict ridden. It turned out that, unbeknownst to her, part of Margie's attraction to and comfort with Paul emanated from his being married. So long as he was married, Margie felt "safe." But once Paul left his marriage, he started making demands that she found herself unable to meet. She had thought she was ready for a commitment, just so long as a commitment was impossible. But when it became possible, Margie felt pressured and ultimately terminated the relationship.

In the long run, it is probably best to leave not for another but for yourself. The decision is not that you would rather be with another than with the first person, but that you would rather be alone than with the first person. The decisions to leave one person and to join another should, if at all possible, be independent, both to take the pressure off the new relationship and to ensure that leaving the first partner was the right decision. Later you can find comfort in knowing that you left because it was right for you rather than because you thought the grass was greener elsewhere, especially if you find that the grass is not actually greener. In ending a close relationship, people generally need to rebuild their sense of self-esteem and independence, and although friends can be helpful, ultimately it is one's own responsibility.

You can be truly successful in your relationship with another only if you have a good relationship with yourself, and often when a relationship with a significant other ends, your relationship with yourself is in need of building and possibly repair. It therefore pays to develop a liking of yourself and to take charge of your own life; once you have rebuilt and created a new and independent life, then look for another from a position of strength. If this all sounds obvious, so it is, but it is nevertheless true, and more difficult to do than to talk about.

This strategy pays off in many ways – not only for the individual, but in helping one attract a better potential partner. People tend not to be attracted to others who are perceived as overly needy or lacking in self-esteem. People generally want to be wanted for themselves, not to help someone get over another relationship, in which case they may be cast aside later.

FORMING A NEW RELATIONSHIP

A mistake that people often make in seeking a new relationship is to look too fast and then try to move the new relationship too quickly. Rapid expression of love and affection often turns other people off, because they feel that they cannot possibly be loved for who they are, but rather only for the image the other has created in his or her mind. Allow yourself the time genuinely to get to know the other so that you, as well as the other, will know that if you express great love or affection, it is because of who the other is rather than because of an image you have built up in your mind. And while you are looking for this new relationship, do your best to see the other as he or she is rather than as you wish him or her to be.

In this period, you may be somewhat desperate and wish to project certain characteristics onto a person that he or she may not have. If you allow yourself enough time, you are less likely to fall into the trap of involving yourself in a rerun of your past relationship, whereby the new person differs from your past partner only in surface characteristics. You are also less likely to look for another person whose main attraction is in being the complete opposite of your former partner. Rather, look with an open mind in your new selection, choosing someone who is right for you, given your needs and wants. Give yourself time to find out who you really are and only then look to become serious with another. Remember also that if you are unhappy with yourself, you cannot expect another to be happy with you. The start of happiness with another is happiness with yourself.

Notes

CHAPTER 1. A THREE-COMPONENT VIEW OF LOVE

1. R. J. Sternberg, *The triangle of love* (New York: Basic, 1988).
2. R. J. Sternberg & S. Grajek, The nature of love, *Journal of Personality and Social Psychology, 55* (1984), 312–329.
3. H. H. Kelley, Analyzing close relationships, in H. H. Kelley et al. (Eds.), *Close relationships* (New York: Freeman, 1983), pp. 20–67.
4. L. B. Rubin, *Just friends* (New York: Harper & Row, 1985).
5. V. J. Derlega, M. Wilson, & A. L. Chaikin, Friendship and disclosure reciprocity, *Journal of Personality and Social Psychology, 34* (1976), 578–582. T. L. Morton, Intimacy and reciprocity of exchange: A comparison of spouses and strangers, *Journal of Personality and Social Psychology, 36* (1978), 72–81. P. C. Cozby, Self-disclosure, reciprocity, and liking, *Sociometry, 35* (1972), 151–160.
6. E. Hatfield & G. W. Walster, *A new look at love* (Reading, MA: Addison-Wesley, 1981).
7. E. Hatfield & G. W. Walster, *A new look at love.*

CHAPTER 2. SEVEN KINDS OF LOVE

1. R. J. Sternberg, *The triangle of love* (New York: Basic, 1988). R. J. Sternberg, A triangular theory of love, *Psychological Review, 93* (1986), 119–135. R. J. Sternberg, Triangulating love, in R. J. Sternberg & M. L. Barnes (Eds.), *The psychology of love* (New Haven, CT: Yale University Press, 1988), pp. 119–138.

2. F. Alberoni, *Falling in love,* trans. L. Venut (New York: Random House, 1983). F. Alberoni, *I love you,* trans. D. H. Newton (Milan: Cooperation Libraria I.V.L.M., 1996).

3. Alberoni, *I love you.*

CHAPTER 3. MANY DIFFERENT TRIANGLES OF LOVE

1. R. J. Sternberg & M. Barnes, Real and ideal others in romantic relationships: Is four a crowd? *Journal of Personality and Social Psychology, 49* (1985), 1586–1608.

2. J. D. Bem, Self-perception theory, *Advances in Experimental Social Psychology, 6* (1972), 1–62.

3. E. Berscheid, Emotion, in H. H. Kelley et al., *Close relationships* (New York: Freeman, 1983), pp. 110–168. G. Mandler, The generation of emotion: A psychological theory, in R. Plutchik and H. Kellerman (Eds.), *Emotion: Theory, research and experience: Vol 1. Theories of emotion* (New York: Academic Press, 1980), pp. 219–243.

4. R. J. Sternberg, Love is a story, *General Psychologist, 31* (1994), 1–11. R. J. Sternberg, Love stories, *Personal Relationships, 3* (1996), 69–70.

5. R. L. Solomon, The opponent-process theory of acquired motivation: The costs of pleasure and the benefits of pain, *American Psychologist, 35* (1980), 691–712.

6. S. Peele & A. Brodsky, *Love and addiction* (New York: New American Library, 1976).

CHAPTER 4. MEASURING THE TRIANGLE OF LOVE

1. R. J. Sternberg, Construct validation of a triangular love scale, *European Journal of Social Psychology, 27* (1997), 313–335.

2. R. J. Sternberg & M. Hojjat, *Empirical tests of aspects of a theory of love as a story* (manuscript submitted for publication).

CHAPTER 5. THE PREHISTORY OF LOVE

1. C. Darwin, *On the origin of species by means of natural selection, or preservation of favoured races in the struggle for life* (London: Murray, 1859).

C. Darwin, *The descent of man and selection in relation to sex* (London: Murray, 1971).

2. H. Spencer, *The principles of psychology* (New York: Appleton, 1886).

3. D. Ackerman, *A natural history of love* (New York: Random House, 1994). D. M. Buss, *The evolution of desire* (New York: Basic, 1994). M. E. Fisher, *Anatomy of love* (New York: Norton, 1992). D. T. Kenrick & M. R. Trost, A reproductive exchange model of heterosexual relationships: Putting proximate economics in ultimate perspective, in C. Hendrick (Ed.), *Close relationships: Review of personality and social psychology* (Newbury Park, CA: Sage, 1989), 10:92–118. M. F. Small, *What's love got to do with it?* (New York: Anchor Books, 1995). G. Wilson, *The Coolidge effect: An evolutionary account of human sexuality* (New York: Morrow, 1981).

4. J. Bowlby, *Attachment and Loss: Vol 1. Attachment* (New York: Basic, 1969).

5. Buss, *The evolution of desire.* R. J. Sternberg, Triangulating love, in R. J. Sternberg & M. L. Barnes (Eds.), *The psychology of love* (New Haven, CT: Yale University Press, 1988), pp. 119–138.

6. D. M. Buss, Sex differences in human mate preferences: Evolutionary hypotheses tested in 87 cultures, *Behavioral and Brain Sciences, 12* (1989), 1–49.

7. Ackerman, *A natural history of love.* I. Singer, *The nature of love* (Chicago: University of Chicago Press, 1987).

8. E. Berscheid & H. T. Reis, Attraction and close relationships, in *Handbook of social psychology,* 4th ed. (New York: McGraw-Hill, 1997). J. A. Howard, P. Blumstein, & P. Swartz, Social or evolutionary theories? Some observations on preferences in human mate selection, *Journal of Personality and Social Psychology, 53* (1987), 194–200.

9. S.W. Gangestad, Sexual selection and physical attractiveness: Implications for mating dynamics, *Human Nature, 4* (1993), 205–235.

10. Gangestad, Sexual selection and physical attractiveness, pp. 205–235.

11. Berscheid, & Reis, Attraction and close relationships.

12. Buss, *The evolution of desire.*

13. Gangestad, Sexual selection and physical attractiveness, pp. 205–235. S. W. Gangestad & D. M. Buss, Pathogen prevalence and human mate preferences, *Ethology and Sociobiology, 14* (1993), 89–96. K. Grammer & R. Thornhill, Human (Homo sapiens) facial attractiveness and sexual selection: The role of symmetry and averageness, *Journal of Personality and Social Psychology, 59* (1994), 1180–1191.

CHAPTER 6. THE HISTORY OF LOVE
REVEALED THROUGH CULTURE

1. P. L. Berger & T. Luckman, *The social construction of reality* (New York: Irvington, 1980).
2. J. R. Averill, The social construction of emotion: With special reference to love, in K. Gergen & K. E. Davis (Eds.), *The social construction of the person* (New York: Springer, 1985). M. S. Davis, *Smut: Erotic reality/obscene ideology* (Chicago: University of Chicago Press, 1983). M. M. Gergen & K. J. Gergen, Attributions, accounts, and close relationships: Close calls and relational resolutions, in J. H. Harvey, T. L. Orbuch, & A. L. Weber (Eds.), *Attributions, accounts, and close relationships* (New York: Springer, 1992).
3. M. Stroebe, M. M. Gergen, K. J. Gergen, & W. Stroebe, Broken hearts or broken bonds: Love and death in historical perspective, *American Psychologist, 47* (1992), 1205–1212.
4. Davis, *Smut.*
5. S. Seidman, The power of desire and the danger of pleasure: Victorian sexuality reconsidered, *Journal of Social History, 24* (1990), 47–67.
6. E. K. Rothman, *Hands and hearts: A history of courtship in America* (Cambridge, MA: Harvard University Press, 1984). P. N. Stearns, Historical analysis in the study of emotion, *Motivation and Emotion, 10* (1986), 185–193.
7. W. T. MacCarey, *Childlike Achilles: Ontogeny and phylogeny in the Iliad* (New York: Columbia University Press, 1982).
8. F. Gonzalez-Reigosa & H. Kaminsky, Greek sexuality, Greek homosexuality, Greek culture: The invention of Apollo, *Psychohistory Review, 17* (1989), 149–181.
9. R. Tannahill, *Sex in history* (London: Sphere, 1989).
10. Tannahill, *Sex in history.*
11. Tannahill, *Sex in history.* S. B. Pomeroy, *Goddesses, whores, wives, and slaves: Women in classical antiquity* (New York: Schocken, 1975).
12. R. Tannahill, *Sex in history.* Pomeroy, *Goddesses, whores, wives, and slaves.*
13. P. G. Brown, Love and marriage in Greek new comedy, *Classical Quarterly, 43* (1993), 189–205.
14. D. Archer, Social deviance, in G. Lindzey & E. Aronson (Eds.), *Handbook of social psychology,* vol. 2 (New York: Random House, 1985).
15. Seidman, The power of desire and the danger of pleasure, pp. 47–67.
16. Rothman, *Hands and hearts.*
17. M. J. Peterson, *Family, love, and work in the lives of Victorian gentlewomen* (Bloomington: Indiana University Press, 1989).

18. K. K. Dion & K. L. Dion, Personality, gender, and the phenomenology of romantic love, in P. Shaver (Ed.), *Review of personality and social psychology: Self, situations, and social behavior,* vol. 6 (Beverly Hills, CA: Sage, 1985). C. Hendrick & S. Hendrick, A theory and method of love, *Journal of Personality and Social Psychology, 50* (1986), 392–402. J. L. Philbrick & J. A. Opolot, Love style: Comparison of African and American attitudes, *Psychological Reports, 46* (1980), 286. J. L. Philbrick & C. R. Stones, Love attitudes in black South Africa: A comparison of school and university students, *Psychological Record, 38* (1988), 249–251. J. L. Philbrick & C. R. Stones, Love attitudes of white South African adolescents, *Psychological Reports, 62* (1988), 17–18. C. R. Stones, Love styles revisited: A cross-national comparison with particular reference to South Africa, *Human Relations, 39* (1986), 379–382. C. R. Stones & J. L. Philbrick, Attitudes toward love among Xhosa University students in South Africa, *Journal of Social Psychology, 129* (1989), 573–575. M. Vandewiele & J. L. Philbrick, Attitudes of Senegalese students toward love, *Psychological Reports, 52* (1983), 915–918.

19. C. H. Simmons, A. V. Kolke, & H. Shimizu, Attitudes toward romantic love among American, German, and Japanese students, *Journal of Social Psychology, 126* (1986), 327–336.

20. K. L. Dion & K. K. Dion, Romantic love: Individual and cultural perspectives, in R. J. Sternberg & M. L. Barnes (Eds.), *The psychology of love* (New Haven, CT: Yale University Press, 1988), pp. 264–289.

21. F. L. K. Hsu, *Americans and Chinese: Passage to difference,* 3rd ed. (Honolulu: University Press of Hawaii, 1989).

22. Hsu, *Americans and Chinese.* R. N. Bellah, R. Madsen, W. M. Sullivan, A. Swidler, & S. M. Tipton, *Habits of the heart* (Berkeley: University of California Press, 1985).

23. Hsu, *Americans and Chinese.*

24. Dion & Dion, Romantic love, pp. 264–289.

25. A. E. Beall & R. J. Sternberg, The social construction of love, *Journal of Social and Personal Relationships, 12* (1995), 417–438. J. A. Gold, R. M. Ryckman, & N. R. Mosley, Romantic mood induction and attraction to a dissimilar other: Is love blind? *Personality and Social Psychology Bulletin, 10* (1984), 358–368. G. L. White, S. Fishbein, & J. Rutstein, Passionate love and the misattribution of arousal, *Journal of Personality and Social Psychology, 41* (1981), 56–62. G. L. White & T. D. Knight, Misattribution of arousal and attraction: Effects of salience of explanations for arousal, *Journal of Experimental Social Psychology, 20* (1984), 55–64.

26. R. J. Sternberg, *The triangle of love* (New York: Basic, 1988).

27. L. A. Kurdek, Relationship quality in gay and lesbian cohabiting couples: A 1-year follow-up study, *Journal of Social and Personal Relationships, 6* (1989), 39–59.

28. M. P. Johnson & L. Leslie, Couple involvement and network structure: A test of dyadic withdrawal hypothesis, *Social Psychology Quarterly, 45* (1982), 34–43.

29. L. A. Peplau & S. L. Gordon, Women and men in love: Gender differences in close heterosexual relationships, in V. E. O'Leary, R. K. Unger, & B. S. Wallston (Eds.), *Women, gender, and social psychology* (Hillsdale, NJ: Erlbaum, 1985).

30. J. D. Douglas & F. C. Atwell, *Love, intimacy and sex* (Newbury Park, CA: Sage, 1988).

31. L. A. Kurdek & P. J. Schmitt, Relationship quality of partners in heterosexual married, heterosexual cohabiting, and gay and lesbian relationships, *Journal of Personality and Social Psychology, 51* 711–720.

32. E. Berscheid, Some comments on love's anatomy: Or, whatever happened to old-fashioned lust? in R. J. Sternberg and M. L. Barnes (Eds.), *The psychology of love* (New Haven, CT: Yale University Press, 1988), pp. 359–374. E. Hatfield, Passionate and companionate love, in R. J. Sternberg and M. L. Barnes (Eds.), *The psychology of love* (New Haven, CT: Yale University Press, 1988), pp. 191–217. R. J. Sternberg, Triangulating love, in R. J. Sternberg and M. L. Barnes (Eds.), *The psychology of love* (New Haven, CT: Yale University Press, 1988), pp. 119–138.

33. C. Cosman, J. Keefe, & K. Weaver (Eds.), *The Penguin book of women poets* (New York: Penguin, 1986), pp. 42, 33.

34. J. W. Critelli, E. J. Myers, & V. E. Loos, The components of love: Romantic attraction and sex role orientation, *Journal of Personality, 54* (1986), 354–370.

35. P. J. Marston, M. L. Hecht, & T. Robers, "True love ways": The subjective experience and communication of romantic love, *Journal of Social and Personal Relationships, 4* (1987), 387–407.

36. Plato, *Symposium,* trans. B. Jowett (Indianapolis: Bobbs-Merrill, 1956).

37. D. M. Buss, Love acts: The evolutionary biology of love, in R. J. Sternberg & M. L. Barnes (Eds.), *The psychology of love* (New Haven, CT: Yale University Press, 1988), pp. 100–118.

38. A. Swidler, Love and adulthood in American culture, in N. J. Smelser & E. H. Erikson (Eds.), *Themes of work and love in adulthood* (Cambridge, MA: Harvard University Press, 1980).

39. S. E. Asch, Studies of independence and conformity: A minority of one against a unanimous majority, *Psychological Monographs, 70* (1956), 9.

M. Sherif, A study of some social factors in perception. *Archives of Psychology, 27* (1935), 187.

40. S. M. Hong, Romantic love, idealistic or pragmatic: Sex differences among Australian young adults, *Psychological Reports, 58* (1986), 922. S. Sprecher & S. Metts, Development of the romantic beliefs scale and examination of the effects of gender and gender-role orientation, *Journal of Social and Personal Relationships, 6* (1989), 387–411.

41. Dion & Dion, Personality, gender, and the phenomenology of romantic love.

42. J. L. Philbrick, Sex differences in romantic attitudes toward love among engineering students, *Psychological Reports, 61* (1987), 482. J. L. Philbrick, F. F. Thomas, G. A. Cretser, & J. Leon, Sex differences in love attitudes of black university students, *Psychological Reports, 62* (1988), 414. J. A. Simpson, B. Campbell, & E. Berscheid, The association between romantic love and marriage: Kephart (1976) twice revisited, *Personality and Social Psychology Bulletin, 12* (1986), 363–372.

43. P. Ries & A. J. Stone, *The American woman, 1992–1993: A status report* (New York: Norton, 1992).

44. A. Swidler, Love and adulthood in American culture, In N. J. Smelser & E. H. Erikson (Eds.), *Themes of work and love in adulthood* (Cambridge, MA: Harvard University Press, 1980).

45. N. Saiedi, *The birth of social theory: Social thought in the Enlightenment and romanticism* (Lanham, MD: University Press of America, 1993).

46. H. Fielding, *History of Tom Jones, a foundling* (London: Oxford University Press, 1974), p. 52.

47. T. Hobbes, *Leviathan* (Harmondsworth, Middlesex: Penguin Books, 1968). B. Spinoza, *Ethics*, trans. A. Boyle (London: Dent, 1989). J. Locke, *An essay concerning human understanding* (London: Oxford University Press, 1975).

48. Spinoza, *Ethics*.

49. Locke, *An essay concerning human understanding*.

50. W. H. McNeill, *History of Western civilization* (Chicago: University of Chicago Press, 1986).

51. R. W. Winks, *Western civilization: A brief history* (Alta Loma, CA: Collegiate, 1988).

52. I. Kant, *Fundamental principles of the metaphysics of morals,* trans. T. K. Abbott (Indianapolis: Bobbs-Merrill, 1949).

53. J. Boswell, *The life of Samuel Johnson* (London: Oxford University Press, 1953).

54. Rothman, *Hands and hearts*.

55. Saiedi, *The birth of social theory.*

56. R. H. Schlegel, Meeting Hume's skeptical challenge, *Review of Metaphysics, 45* (1992), 691–711.

57. F. M. A. Voltaire, *Candide and other writings* (New York: Modern Library, 1956).

58. B. Fehr, How do I love thee? Let me consult my prototype, in S. W. Duck (Ed.), *Individuals in relationships [Understanding relationships processes 1]* (Newbury Park, CA: Sage, 1993).

59. Rothman, *Hands and hearts.*

60. Rothman, *Hands and hearts.*

61. J. D'Emilio & E. B. Freedman, *Intimate matters* (New York: Harper & Row, 1988).

62. N. H. Frijda, *The emotions* (Cambridge: Cambridge University Press, 1986).

63. A. Feingold, Matching for attractiveness in romantic partners and same-sex friends: A meta-analysis and theoretical critique, *Psychological Bulletin, 104* (1988), 226–235.

64. S. Kiesler & R. Baral, The search for a romantic partner: The effects of self-esteem and physical attractiveness on romantic behavior, in K. J. Gergen & D. Marlowe (Eds.), *Personality and social behavior* (Reading, MA: Addison-Wesley, 1970).

65. K. K. McClanahan, J. A. Gold, E. Lenney, R. M. Ryckman, & G. E. Kulberg, Infatuation and attraction to a dissimilar other: Why is love blind? *Journal of Social Psychology, 130* (1990), 433–445.

66. D. J. Johnson & C. E. Rusbult, Resisting temptation: Devaluation of alternative partners as a means of maintaining commitment in close relationships, *Journal of Personality and Social Psychology, 57* (1989), 967–980.

67. A. Aron, D. G. Dutton, E. N. Aron, & A. Iverson, Experiences of falling in love. *Journal of Social and Personal Relationships, 6* (1989), 243–257.

68. L. A. Peplau & S. L. Gordon, Women and men in love: Gender differences in close heterosexual relationships, in V. E. O'Leary, R. K. Unger, & B. S. Wallston (Eds.), *Women, gender, and social psychology* (Hillsdale, NJ: Erlbaum, 1985).

69. M. R. Parks, C. M. Stan, & L. L. Eggert, Romantic involvement and social network involvement, *Social Psychology Quarterly, 46* (1983), 116–131.

70. R. Buck, Emotional communication in personal relationships: A developmental-interactionist view, in C. Hendrick (Ed.), *Close relationships. Review of personality and social psychology,* vol. 10 (Newbury Park, CA: Sage Publications, 1989).

CHAPTER 7. THE HISTORY OF LOVE
REVEALED THROUGH LITERATURE

1. J. Grimm & W. Grimm, *German folk tales,* trans. F. P. Magom & A. Krappe (Carbondale: Southern Illinois University Press, 1960).
2. Grimm & Grimm, *German folk tales.*
3. W. Shakespeare, *The tragedy of Othello,* in W. Cross & T. Brooke (Eds.), *The Yale Shakespeare* (New York: Barnes & Noble, 1993).
4. W. Shakespeare, *Love's labour's lost,* in W. Cross & T. Brooke (Eds.), *The Yale Shakespeare* (New York: Barnes & Noble, 1993).
5. A. Jablow, *Yes and no: The intimate folklore of Africa* (Westport, CT: Greenwood, 1961).
6. D. Wolkstein, *The first love stories: From Isis and Osiris to Tristan and Iseult* (New York: HarperCollins, 1991).
7. R. Erdoes & A. Ortiz, (Eds.), *American Indian myths and legends* (New York: Pantheon, 1984).
8. *New Oxford annotated Bible with the Apocrypha* (Oxford: Oxford University Press, 1973).
9. R. J. Sternberg, *The triangle of love* (New York: Basic, 1988).
10. Wolkstein, *The first love stories.*
11. E. Hatfield & S. Sprecher, *Mirror, mirror: The importance of looks in everyday life* (Albany: State University of New York Press, 1986).
12. J. A. B. Van Buitenen, *Tales of ancient India* (Chicago: University of Chicago Press, 1959).
13. L. Esquivel, *Like water for chocolate,* trans. C. Christensen & T. Christensen (New York: Doubleday, 1992).
14. S. Thompson, *Tales of the North American Indians* (Bloomington: Indiana University Press, 1966).
15. Y.-L. C. Chin, Y. S. Center, & M. Ross, *Traditional Chinese folktales* (Armonk, NY: M. E. Sharpe, 1989).
16. J. Onassis (Ed.), *The firebird and other Russian fairy tales* (New York: Viking, 1978).
17. Grimm & Grimm, *German folk tales.*
18. Erdoes & Ortiz, *American Indian myths and legends.*
19. Van Buitenen, *Tales of ancient India.*
20. Vatsyayana, *The Kama Sutra of Vatsyayana,* trans. R. Burton (New York: Dorset, 1962).
21. Vatsyayana, *The Kama Sutra of Vatsyayana.*
22. Van Buitenen, *Tales of ancient India.*
23. Vatsyayana, *The Kama Sutra of Vatsyayana.*

24. A. Marvell, Selected poems, in A. Alexander, H. Barrows, C. Blake, A. Carr, A. Eastman, & H. English (Eds.), *The Norton anthology of poetry* (New York: Norton, 1983).

25. G. Garcia Marquez, *Love in the time of cholera* (New York: Knopf, 1988).

26. A. Marshall, *People of the dreamtime* (Melbourne: Hyland House, 1978).

27. *New Oxford annotated Bible with the Apocrypha* (Oxford: Oxford University Press, 1973).

28. Garcia Marquez, *Love in the time of cholera.*

29. Wolkstein, *The first love stories.*

30. J. W. Spellman, Preface, in Vatsyayana, *The Kama Sutra of Vatsyayana,* trans. R. Burton, (New York: Dorset, 1962).

31. Jablow, *Yes and no.*

32. Chin, Center, & Ross, *Traditional Chinese folktales.*

33. Wolkstein, *The first love stories.*

34. Wolkstein, *The first love stories.*

35. Wolkstein, *The first love stories.*

36. Vatsyayana, *The Kama Sutra of Vatsyayana.*

37. Wolkstein, *The first love stories.*

38. T. Bullfinch, *Bullfinch's mythology* (New York: Thomas Crowell, 1947).

39. Ovid, *Ars amatoria,* trans. F. A. Wright (London: Routledge, 1929).

40. Vatsyayana, *The Kama Sutra of Vatsyayana.*

41. W. Shakespeare, *Romeo and Juliet.* in W. Cross & T. Brooke (Eds.), *The Yale Shakespeare* (New York: Barnes & Noble, 1993).

42. W. Shakespeare, *A midsummer night's dream,* in W. Cross & T. Brooke (Eds.), *The Yale Shakespeare* (New York: Barnes & Noble, 1993).

43. Kalidasa. *Shakuntala and other writings,* trans. A. Ryder (New York: Dutton, 1959).

44. B. Stevenson, *The Macmillan book of proverbs, maxims, and famous phrases* (New York: Macmillan, 1968).

45. D. de Rougement, *Love in the Western world,* trans. M. Belgion (New York: Pantheon, 1956).

46. Wolkstein, *The first love stories.*

47. G. Garcia Marquez, *Love in the time of cholera.*

48. *New Oxford annotated Bible with the Apocrypha.*

49. Spellman, Preface.

50. W. Shakespeare, *The tragedy of Antony and Cleopatra,* in W. Cross & T. Brooke (Eds.), *The Yale Shakespeare* (New York: Barnes & Noble, 1993).

51. E. Hamilton, *Mythology* (Boston: Little, Brown, 1942).

52. Chin, Center, & Ross, *Traditional Chinese folktales.*

53. Wolkstein, *The first love stories.*
54. Kalidasa, *Shakuntala and other writings.*
55. A. Bradstreet, Selected poems, in A. Alexander, H. Barrows, C. Blake, A. Carr, A. Eastman, & H. English (Eds.), *The Norton anthology of poetry* (New York: Norton, 1983).
56. Wolkstein, *The first love stories.*
57. Wolkstein, *The first love stories.*
58. Bullfinch, *Bullfinch's mythology.*
59. Erdoes & Ortiz, *American Indian myths and legends.*
60. Hamilton, *Mythology.*
61. Garcia Marquez, *Love in the time of cholera.*
62. Shakespeare, *Romeo and Juliet.*
63. Wolkstein, *The first love stories.*
64. Dante, *The divine comedy* (Manchester: Carcanet New Press, 1980).
65. Spellman, Preface.
66. Garcia Marquez, *Love in the time of cholera.*
67. Garcia Marquez, *Love in the time of cholera.*
68. E. B. Browning, Selected poems, in A. Alexander, H. Barrows, C. Blake, A. Carr, A. Eastman, & H. English (Eds.), *The Norton anthology of poetry* (New York: Norton, 1983).
69. S. Sanchez, Just don't never give up on love, in L. Goss & M. E. Barnes (Eds.), *Talk that talk: An anthology of African-American storytelling* (New York: Simon & Schuster, 1989).
70. Spellman, Preface.
71. Marshall, *People of the dreamtime.*
72. Homer, *The odyssey,* trans. T. E. Lawrence (New York: Oxford University Press, 1991).
73. Bullfinch, *Bullfinch's mythology.*
74. *New Oxford annotated Bible with the Apocrypha.*
75. R. Tyler (Ed. and Trans.), *Japanese tales.* (New York: Pantheon, 1987).
76. Hamilton, *Mythology.*
77. G. Chaucer, *The Canterbury tales* (New York: Norton, 1971).
78. W. Shakespeare, *As you like it,* in W. Cross & T. Brooke (Eds.), *The Yale Shakespeare* (New York: Barnes & Noble, 1993).
79. Shakespeare, *A midsummer night's dream.*
80. Rougement, *Love in the Western world.*
81. Erdoes & Ortiz, *American Indian myths and legends.*
82. Wolkstein, *The first love stories.*
83. G. von Strassburg, *Tristan* (Stuttgart: Philipp Reclam Jun, 1993).
84. *New Oxford annotated Bible with the Apocrypha.*

85. W. Shakespeare, (1993). Sonnets, in W. Cross & Tucker Brooke (Eds.), *The Yale Shakespeare* (New York: Barnes & Noble, 1993).
86. Wolkstein, *The first love stories.*
87. Shakespeare, Sonnets.
88. R. Herrick, Selected poems, in A. Alexander, H. Barrows, C. Blake, A. Carr, A. Eastman, & H. English (Eds.), *The Norton anthology of poetry* (New York: Norton, 1983).
89. Marvell, Selected poems.
90. G. Flaubert, *Madame Bovary* (Paris: Garnier, 1971).
91. Stevenson, *The Macmillan book of proverbs, maxims, and famous phrases.*
92. Grimm & Grimm, *German folk tales.*
93. Thompson, *Tales of the North American Indians.*
94. Aeschylus, *Oresteia,* trans. R. Fagles (New York: Penguin, 1983).
95. Euripides, *Medea,* trans. D. Egan (Laurinburg, NC: St. Andrews Press, 1991).
96. *New Oxford annotated Bible with the Apocrypha.*
97. Wolkstein, *The first love stories.*
98. J. Koram, The lion and the Ashiko drum: A fable from South Carolina, in L. Goss & M. E. Barnes (Eds.), *Talk that talk: An anthology of African-American storytelling* (New York: Simon & Schuster, 1989).
99. R. J. Sternberg, *Love is a story* (New York: Oxford University Press, 1998).

CHAPTER 8. THE ROLE OF CHILDHOOD AND ADOLESCENCE

1. D. M. Buss, *The evolution of desire* (New York: Basic, 1994).
2. M. D. S. Ainsworth, M. C. Blehar, E. Waters, & S. Wall, *Patterns of attachment: Assessed in the strange situation and at home* (Hillsdale, NJ: Erlbaum, 1978).
3. D. Benoit & K. C. H. Parker, Stability and transmission of attachment across three generations, *Child Development, 65* (1994), 1444–1456. P. Fonagy, H. Steele, & M. Steele, Maternal representations of attachment during pregnancy predict the organization of infant–mother attachment at one year, *Child Development, 62* (1991), 891–905. M. Main, N. Kaplan, & J. Cassidy, Security in infancy, childhood, and adulthood: A move to the level of representation, *Monographs of the Society for Research in Child Development, 50* (1–2, Serial No. 209) (1985), pp. 66–104.
4. J. Elicker, M. Englund, & L. A. Sroufe, Predicting peer competence and peer relationships in childhood from early parent–child relationships, in R. D. Parke & G. W. Lass (Eds.), *Family-peer relationships: Modes of link-*

age (Hillsdale, NJ: Erlbaum, 1992), pp. 77–106. C. Hazan & P. Shaver, Romantic love conceptualized as an attachment process, *Journal of Personality and Social Psychology, 52* (1987), 511–524.

5. Hazan & Shaver, Romantic love conceptualized as an attachment process, pp. 511–524. C. Hazan & P. Shaver, Attachment as an organizational framework for research on close relationships, *Psychological Inquiry, 5* (1994), 1–22.

6. K. Bartholomew & L. M. Horowitz, Attachment styles among young adults: A test of a four-category model, *Journal of Personality and Social Psychology, 61* (1991), 226–244.

7. K. Grossman, K. E. Grossman, S. Spangler, G. Suress, & L. Unzner, Maternal sensitivity and newborn attachment orientation responses as related to quality of attachment in Northern Germany, *Monographs of the Society for Research in Child Development, 50* (1–2, Serial No. 209) (1985). A. Sagi, M. E. Lamb, K. S. Lewkowicz, R. Shoham, R. Dvir, & D. Estes, Security of infant–mother, –father, and metaplet attachments among kibbutz reared Israeli children, *Monographs of the Society for Research in Child Development, 50* (1–2, Serial No. 209) (1985). K. Miyake, S. Chen, & J. J. Campos, Infant temperament, mother's mode of interaction, and attachment in Japan. An interim report, *Monographs of the Society for Research in Child Development, 50* (1–2, Serial No. 209) (1985).

8. M. W. Baldwin, B. Fehr, E. Keedian, M. Seidel, & D. W. Thomson, An exploration of the relational schemata underlying attachment styles: Self-report and lexical decisions approaches, *Personality and Social Psychology Bulletin, 19* (1993), 746–754.

9. M. D. S. Ainsworth, Attachment: Retrospect and prospect, in C. M. Parkes & J. Stevenson Hinde (Eds.), *The place of attachment in human behavior* (New York: Basic, 1982).

10. R. J. Sternberg, *Thinking styles* (Cambridge: Cambridge University Press, 1997).

11. R. J. Sternberg, *The triangle of love* (New York: Basic, 1988).

CHAPTER 9. THE ROLE OF ADULTHOOD

1. E. Berscheid & E. Walster, Physical attractiveness, in L. Berkowitz (Ed.), *Advances in experimental social psychology,* vol. 7 (New York: Academic, 1974). K. K. Dion, E. Berscheid, & E. Walster, What is beautiful is good, *Journal of Personality and Social Psychology, 24* (1972), 285–290.

2. A. H. Eagly, R. D. Ashomore, M. G. Makhaijani, & L. C. Longo, What

is beautiful is good, but . . .: A meta analytic review of research on the physical attractiveness stereotype, *Psychological Bulletin, 110* (1991), 109–128.

3. F. Diener, B. Wolsic, & F. Fujita, Physical attractiveness and subjective well-being. *Journal of Personality and Social Psychology, 69* (1995), 120–129. D. S. Hamermesh & J. E. Biddle, Beauty and the labor market. *American Economic Review, 84* (1994), 1174–1195.

4. F. Diener, B. Wolsic, & F. Fujita, Physical attractiveness and subjective well-being, pp. 120–129.

5. M. R. Cunningham, A. R. Roberts, A. P. Barbee, P. B. Druen, & C. Wu, "Their ideas of beauty are, on the whole, the same as ours": Consistency and variability in the cross-cultural perception of female physical attractiveness, *Journal of Personality and Social Psychology, 68* (1995), 261–279.

6. M. C. Alicke, R. H. Smith, & M. L. Klotz, Judgments of physical attractiveness: The role of faces and bodies, *Personality and Social Psychology Bulletin, 12* (1986), 381–389. Cunningham et al., "Their ideas of beauty are, on the whole, the same as ours," pp. 261–279.

7. J. H. Langlois & L. A. Roggman, Attractive faces are only average, *Psychological Science, 1* (1990), 115–121. J. H. Langlois, L. A. Roggman, & L. Musselman, What is average and what is not average about attractive faces. *Psychological Science, 5* (1994), 214–220.

8. E. Walster, V. Aronson, D. Abrahams, & L. Rottmann, Importance of physical attractiveness in dating behavior, *Journal of Personality and Social Psychology, 4* (1966), 508–516.

9. E. Berscheid, K. Dion, E. Walster, & G. W. Walster, Physical attractiveness and dating choice: A test of the matching hypothesis, *Journal of Experimental Social Psychology, 7* (1971), 173–189.

10. B. I. Murstein, Physical attraction and marital choice. *Journal of Personality and Social Psychology, 22* (1972), 8–12. B. I. Murstein, *Who will marry whom?* (New York: Springer, 1976).

11. Dion, Berscheid, & Walster, What is beautiful is good, pp. 285–290.

12. H. Sigall, & D. Landy, Radiating beauty: The effects of having a physically attractive partner on person perception, *Journal of Personality and Social Psychology, 28* (1973), 218–224.

13. D. Landy and H. Sigall, Beauty is talent: Task evaluation as a function of the performer's physical attractiveness, *Journal of Personality and Social Psychology, 29* (1974), 299–304.

14. D. Bar-Tal & L. Saxe, Perceptions of similarly and dissimilarly attractive

couples and individuals, *Journal of Personality and Social Psychology, 33* (1976), 772–781.

15. Berscheid et al., Physical attractiveness and dating choice: A test of the matching hypothesis, pp. 173–189.

16. M. Snyder, E. Berscheid, & P. Glick, Focusing on the exterior and the interior: Two investigations of the initiation of personal relationships, *Journal of Personality and Social Psychology, 48* (1985), 1427–1439.

17. Snyder, Berscheid, & Glick, Focusing on the exterior and the interior, pp. 1427–1439.

18. D. G. Dutton & A. P. Aron, Some evidence for heightened sexual attraction under conditions of high anxiety, *Journal of Personality and Social Psychology, 30* (1974), 510–517.

19. Dutton & Aron, Some evidence for heightened sexual attraction under conditions of high anxiety, pp. 510–517.

20. C. T. Hill, Z. Rubin, & L. A. Peplau, Breakups before marriage: The end of 103 affairs, *Journal of Social Issues, 32* (1976), 147–167.

21. R. J. Sternberg, *The triangle of love* (New York: Basic, 1988).

22. Sternberg, *The triangle of love.*

23. L. Festinger, S. Schachter, & K. W. Back, *Social pressures in informal groups: A study of human factors in housing* (New York: Harper, 1950).

24. T. M. Newcomb, *The acquaintance process* (New York: Holt, Rinehart, & Winston, 1961).

25. M. W. Segal, Alphabet and attraction: An unobtrusive measure of the effect of propinquity in a field setting. *Journal of Personality and Social Psychology, 30* (1974), 654–657.

26. R. B. Zajonc, Attitudinal effects of mere exposure, *Journal of Personality and Social Psychology Monograph Supplement, 9* (1968), 1–27.

27. S. Saegert, W. Swap, & R. B. Zajonc, Exposure, context, and interpersonal attraction, *Journal of Personality and Social Psychology, 25* (1973), 234–242.

28. E. B. Ebbesen, G. L. Kjos, & V. J. Konecni, Spatial ecology: Its effects on the choice of friends and enemies, *Journal of Experimental Social Psychology, 12* (1976), 505–518.

29. E. L. Hartley, *Problems in prejudice* (New York: King's Crown, 1946).

30. C. W. Backman & P. F. Secord, The effect of perceived liking on interpersonal attraction, *Human Relations, 12* (1959), 379–384.

31. R. E. Stapleton, P. Nacci, & J. T. Tedeschi, Interpersonal attraction and the reciprocation of benefits, *Journal of Personality and Social Psychology, 28* (1973), 199–205.

32. M. Worthy, A. L. Gary, & G. M. Kahn, Disclosure as an exchange process, *Journal of Personality and Social Psychology, 13* (1969), 59–63.

33. E. W. Burgess & P. Wallin, *Engagement and marriage* (Philadelphia: Lippincott, 1953).

34. A. Skolnick, Married lives: Longitudinal perspectives on marriage, in D. H. Eichorn, J. A. Clausen, N. Haan, M. P. Honzik, & P. H. Mussen (Eds.), *Present and past in middle life* (New York: Academic, 1981).

35. D. Byrne, *The attraction paradigm* (New York: Academic, 1971). A. Tesser & M. Brodie, A note on the evaluation of a "computer date," *Psychonomic Science, 23* (1971), 300.

36. Byrne, *The attraction paradigm*. A. Tesser & M. Brodie, A note on the evaluation of a "computer date," p. 300.

37. T. L. Huyston & G. Levinger, Interpersonal attraction and relationships, in M. R. Rosenzweig & L. W. Perter (Eds.), *Annual Review of Psychology*, vol. 29 (Palo Alto, CA: Annual Review, 1978).

38. W. B. Swann, Jr. To be adored or to be known: The interplay of self enhancement and self verification, in R. M. Sorrentino & E. T. Higgins (Eds.), *Motivation and cognition* (New York: Guilford, 1990), 2:408–488.

39. R. Driscoll, K. W. Davis, & M. E. Lipetz, Parental interference and romantic love, *Journal of Personality and Social Psychology, 24* (1972), 1–10.

40. E. Walster, G. W. Walster, J. Piliavin, & L. Schmidt, Playing hard-to-get: Understanding an elusive phenomenon, *Journal of Personality and Social Psychology, 26* (1973), 113–121.

41. J. W. Brehm, *A theory of psychological reactance* (New York: Academic, 1966). S. S. Brehm & J. W. Brehm, *A theory of freedom and control* (New York: Academic, 1981).

42. Sternberg, *The triangle of love*.

43. Byrne, *The attraction paradigm*.

44. R. F. Winch, *Mate selection: A theory of complementary needs* (New York: Harper, 1958). H. A. Murray, *Explorations in personality* (New York: Oxford University Press, 1938).

45. T. L. Morton, Intimacy and reciprocity of exchange: A comparison of spouses and strangers, *Journal of Personality and Social Psychology, 36* (1978), 72–81. H. T. Reis & P. Shaver, Intimacy as an interpersonal process, in S. W. Duck (Ed.), *Handbook of personal relationships* (Chichester: Wiley, 1988), pp. 367–389.

46. N. L. Collins & L. C. Miller, Self-disclosure and liking: A meta-analytic review, *Psychological Bulletin, 116* (1994), 457–475.

47. C. B. Wortman, P. Adesman, E. Herman, & R. Greenberg, Self-disclosure: An attributional perspective, *Journal of Personality and Social Psychol-*

ogy, 33 (1976), 184–191. E. E. Jones & R. L. Archer, Are there special effects of personalistic self-disclosure? *Journal of Experimental Social Psychology, 12* (1976), 180–193.

48. Reis & Shaver, Intimacy as an interpersonal process, pp. 367–389.
49. A. Tesser, M. Millar, & J. Moore, Some affective consequences of social comparison and reflection processes: The pain and pleasure of being close, *Journal of Personality and Social Psychology, 54* (1988), 49–61.
50. A. C. Kerckhoff & K. E. Davis, Value consensus and need complementarity in mate selection, *American Sociological Review, 27* (1962), 295–303.
51. G. Levinger, D. J. Senn, & B. W. Jorgensen, Progress toward permanence in courtship: A test of the Kerckhoff-Davis hypotheses, *Sociometry, 33* (1970), 427–443.
52. B. I. Murstein, Stimulus-value-role: A theory of marital choice, *Journal of Marriage and the Family, 32* (1970), 465–481.
53. R. A. Lewis, A developmental framework for the analysis of premarital dyadic formation, *Family Process, 11* (1972), 17–48.
54. S. Freud, Certain neurotic mechanisms in jealousy, paranoia, and homosexuality, in *Collected papers,* vol. 2 (London: Hogarth, 1992).
55. T. Reik, *A psychologist looks at love* (New York: Farrar & Rinehart, 1944).
56. M. Klein & J. Riviere, *Love, hate, and reparation* (London: Hogarth, 1953).
57. A. H. Maslow, *Motivation and personality* (New York: Harper & Row, 1954).
58. Maslow, *Motivation and personality.*
59. Maslow, *Motivation and personality.*
60. J. A. Lee, A typology of styles of loving, *Personality and Social Psychology Bulletin, 3* (1977), 173–182. R. J. Sternberg, Triangulating love, in R. J. Sternberg & M. L. Barnes (Eds.), *The psychology of love* (New Haven, CT: Yale University Press, 1988), pp. 119–138.
61. M. Lasswell & N. M. Lobsenz, *Styles of loving* (New York: Ballantine, 1980).
62. C. Hendrick & S. S. Hendrick, A theory and method of love, *Journal of Personality and Social Psychology, 50* (1986), 392–402. C. Hendrick & S. S. Hendrick, Research on love: Does it measure up?, *Journal of Personality and Social Psychology, 56* (1989), 784–794. C. Hendrick & S. S. Hendrick, *Romantic love* (Newbury Park, CA: Sage, 1992).

CHAPTER 10. THE ROLE OF REWARD

1. A. J. Lott & B. E. Lott, Group cohesiveness, communication level, and conformity, *Journal of Abnormal and Social Psychology, 62* (1961),

408–412. A. J. Lott & B. E. Lott, The role of reward in the formation of positive interpersonal attitudes, in T. L. Huston (Ed.), *Foundations of interpersonal attraction* (New York: Academic, 1974).

2. A. J. Lott & B. E. Lott, A learning theory approach to interpersonal attitudes, in A. G. Greenwald & T. M. Ostrom (Eds.), *Psychological foundations of attitudes* (New York: Academic, 1968).

3. W. Griffitt & R. Veitch, Hot and crowded: Influence of population density and temperature on interpersonal affective behavior, *Journal of Personality and Social Psychology, 17* (1971), 92–98.

4. G. L. Clore & D. Byrne, A reinforcement-affect model of attraction, in T. L. Huston (Ed.), *Foundations of interpersonal attraction* (New York: Academic, 1974).

5. S. S. Brehm, *Intimate relationships* (New York: Random House, 1985).

6. G. C. Homans, *Social behavior: Its elementary forms,* rev. ed. (New York: Harcourt Brace Jovanovich, 1974). B. F. Skinner, *Science and human behavior* (New York: Macmillan, 1953).

7. E. Walster, G. W. Walster, & E. Berscheid, *Equity: Theory and research* (Boston: Allyn & Bacon, 1978).

CHAPTER 11. THE COURSE OF RELATIONSHIPS

1. I. Altman & D. A. Taylor, *Social penetration: The development of interpersonal relationships* (New York: Holt Rinehart & Winston, 1973).

2. Z. Rubin, Measurement of romantic love, *Journal of Personality and Social Psychology, 16* (1970), 265–273.

3. Z. Rubin, Measurement of romantic love, pp. 265–273.

4. C. T. Hill, Z. Rubin, & L. A. Peplau, Breakups before marriage: The end of 103 affairs, *Journal of Social Issues, 32* (1976), 147–167.

5. R. J. Sternberg, *The triangle of love* (New York: Basic, 1988), chap. 6.

6. Sternberg, *The triangle of love,* chap. 6.

CHAPTER 12. DECAY OF RELATIONSHIPS

1. R. S. Cimbalo, V. Faling, & P. Mousaw, The course of love: A cross-sectional design, *Psychological Reports, 38* (1976), 1292–1294.

2. P. C. Pineo, Disenchantment in the later years of marriage, *Marriage and Family Living, 23* (1961), 3–11.

3. W. G. Graziano & L. M. Musser, The joining and the parting of the ways,

in S. Duck (Ed.), *Personal Relationships: Vol. 4. Dissolving Relationships* (New York: Academic, 1982).

4. E. Berscheid & H. Reis, Attraction and close relationships, in *The handbook of social psychology,* 4th ed. (New York: McGraw-Hill, 1997).

5. J. D. Teachman & K. A. Polonko, Cohabitation and marital stability in the United States, *Social Forces, 69* (1990), 207–220.

6. R. W. Levenson, L. L. Carstensen, & J. M. Gottman, The influence of age and gender on affect, physiology, and their interrelations: A study of long term marriages, *Journal of Personality and Social Psychology, 67* (1994), 56–68. N. D. Glenn, Quantitative research on marital quality in the 1980's: A critical review, *Journal of Marriage and the Family, 52* (1990), 818–831.

7. Glenn, Quantitative research on marital quality in the 1980's, pp. 818–831.

8. S. S. Brehm, *Intimate relationships* (New York: Random House, 1985).

9. B. R. Orvis, H. H. Kelley, & D. Butler, Attributional conflict in young couples, in J. H. Harvey, W. J. Ickes, & R. E. Kidd (Eds.), *New direction in attribution research,* vol. 1 (Hillsdale, NJ: Erlbaum, 1976).

10. E. Berscheid, W. Graziano, T. Monson, & M. Dermer, Outcome dependency: Attention, attribution, and attraction, *Journal of Personality and Social Psychology, 34* (1976), 978–989. T. W. Smith & S. S. Brehm, Person perception and the Type A coronary-prone behavior pattern, *Journal of Personality and Social Psychology, 40* (1981), 1137–1149.

11. Berscheid et al., Outcome dependency: Attention, attribution, and attraction, pp. 978–989. Smith & Brehm, Person perception and the Type A coronary-prone behavior pattern, pp. 1137–1149.

12. H. H. Kelley, An application of attribution theory to research methodology for close relationships, in G. Levinger & H. L. Raush (Eds.), *Close relationships: Perspectives on the meaning of intimacy* (Amherst: University of Massachusetts Press, 1977).

13. W. J. Doherty, Cognitive processes in intimate conflict: I. Extending attribution theory, *American Journal of Family Therapy, 9* (1981), 1–13. H. H. Kelley, *Personal relationships: Their structures and processes* (Hillsdale, NJ: Erlbaum, 1979).

14. W. J. Doherty, Attribution style and negative problem solving in marriage, *Family Relation, 31* (1982), 201–205.

15. Doherty, Attribution style and negative problem solving in marriage, pp. 201–205.

16. F. Fincham & K. D. O'Leary, Casual inferences for spouse behavior in maritally distressed and nondistressed couples, *Journal of Clinical and Social Psychology, 1* (1983), 42–57.

17. Graziano & Musser, The joining and the parting of the ways.
18. N. S. Jacobson, D. W. McDonald, W. C. Follette, & R. A. Berley, Attributional processes in distressed and nondistressed married couples, *Cognitive Therapy and Research, 9* (1985), 35–50.
19. N. S. Jacobson, W. C. Follette, & D. W. McDonald, Reactivity to positive and negative behavior in distressed and nondistressed married couples, *Journal of Consulting and Clinical Psychology, 50* (1982), 706–714.
20. R. W. Levenson & J. M. Gottman, Physiological and affective predictors of change in relationship satisfaction, *Journal of Personality and Social Psychology, 49* (1985), 85–94. J. M. Gottman & R. W. Levenson, Marital processes predictive of later dissolution: Behavior, physiology, and health, *Journal of Personality and Social Psychology, 63* (1992), 221–233.
21. J. M. Gottman, The roles of conflict engagement, escalation, and avoidance in marital interaction: A longitudinal view of five types of couples, *Journal of Consulting and Clinical Psychology, 61* (1993), 6–15. J. M. Gottman, *What predicts divorce? The relationships between marital processes and marital outcomes* (Hillsdale, NJ: Erlbaum, 1994).
22. F. J. Floyd & H. J. Markman, Observational biases in spouse observation: Toward a cognitive/behavioral model of marriage, *Journal of Consulting and Clinical Psychology, 51* (1993), 450–457.
23. R. J. Sternberg, *The triangle of love* (New York: Basic, 1988).
24. T. L. Huston & A. F. Chorost, Behavioral buffers on the effect of negativity on marital satisfaction: A longitudinal study, *Personal Relationships, 1* (1994), 223–239.
25. J. M. Gottman, *Marital interaction: Experimental investigations* (New York: Academic, 1979).
26. Sternberg, *The triangle of love.*
27. R. J. Sternberg, *Love the way you want it* (New York: Bantam, 1991).
28. E. E. Filsinger & S. J. Thoma, Behavioral antecedents of relationship stability and adjustment: A five year longitudinal study, *Journal of Marriage and the Family, 50* (1988), 785–795.

CHAPTER 13. DISSOLUTION OF AND
NEW BEGINNINGS FOR RELATIONSHIPS

1. D. Vaughan, *Uncoupling* (New York: Oxford University Press, 1986).
2. R. Weiss, *Marital separation* (New York: Basic, 1975).
3. R. J. Sternberg, *The triangle of love* (New York: Basic, 1988).
4. R. J. Sternberg, *Love the way you want it* (New York: Bantam, 1991).

Index

203